The
Guidebook to
HAPPINESS

Are You Leaving Your Happiness to Chance?
Learn Proven & Practical Solutions for
Experiencing Real Happiness

Carl Massy

Dedication

To all of the amazing teachers I have had the great fortune to learn from and share experiences with — thank you for continuing to share your wisdom with me.

And to my amazing partner, Ferry.

CONTENTS

Recommended reference material

An introduction:
Who is Carl Massy?

When I look back over my life so far, there is an intriguing grand design to it all. Although I could have done without a few of the bumps and bruises along the way, I know they were all part of the sculpting process and have played a role in who I am today. I have been an Australian Army Major, an international security consultant to the Olympic Games and, after fulfilling a long-standing desire, inspired by the big-headed, big-hearted Tony Robbins, I am now a Neuro Linguistics Life Coach and the proud owner of WorldsBIGGESTGym™, which is based on the idea that the greatest workout we do every day is actually going on in our minds. But more on that later.

Not only once upon a time but numerous times in my late teens and well into my twenties, I acted like an absolute dill. Americans might translate 'dill' as 'pain in the butt'; in the Queen's English you might say I was a 'confused and misunderstood young gentleman'. Whichever way you choose to phrase it, I was not a model human being and I was not doing myself any favors. Granted there were times when it was very entertaining for others to watch me in a drunken state doing backward somersaults off the bar; but the experience of crawling to the hospital afterwards because I had almost fractured both my heels was much less enjoyable, not to mention excruciatingly painful and somewhat embarrassing.

After a particularly boozy night with me and my 29-year-old drinking buddies (that would be me, myself and I), I found myself watching an infomercial at about 2am on a Sunday when this guy with an enormous head and a frame to match and a grin from ear to ear was talking about 'transformation'. He was big enough, bold enough and loud enough to penetrate my mental haze and I ended up ordering a program from the American Success Coach Tony Robbins. This was my wake-up call. It was the right person, saying the right thing, in the right way, and at the right time.

That was Easter 1999. From then on, the journey to my new life began in earnest. I dove into learning about the integration of body and mind with Neuro Linguistic Programming (NLP), hypnosis, Reiki and physical training and devoted my time to reading and researching and made plenty of discoveries along the way. I figured out something that had been staring me in the face all along: *I only knew what I knew*. Revelation number one!

Have you ever tried to fix the engine on a car when you did not have a User's Manual, had never been shown how, had no one there to help you, and really didn't know what it was supposed to sound like in the end? I was working with the best resources I had at the time, but those resources were sorely lacking. When I talk about 'resources' I am talking about role models (past and present), teachers (past and present) and the beliefs and behaviors I had adopted in my formative years, which formed the software programs in my mind and were effectively running the show. *Don't worry about understanding all of this now. I will be talking a lot more about the programs that are playing in our mind and whether they are serving us or sentencing us*. There was a very good chance that if I continued to live this way I would never get the engine of my life performing at its maximum capability.

As I merged 20 years of strategic planning expertise with my study of happiness, I came to realize that there are plenty of things we choose to do, or not do, that make a huge impact on the quality of our life experience.

That was revelation number two! I had thought I was just unlucky. In fact, that was what I had chosen to believe. I was an expert at blaming my 'bad luck':

for being arrested for 'disorderly behavior' in my early twenties; or for being paraded before my Commanding Officer and told that if I did not drastically improve my performance over the next few months I would be asked to justify why I should be kept in the unit; plus plenty of other 'bad luck' incidents.

It wasn't that I had been unlucky — I had just been making really bad choices — no one had forced me to get into the situations I was in. Revelation number two taught me that I lacked the good sense, self-belief and courage to make better choices. I needed to build up trust in myself and gain the courage to say 'no' if I knew that something was likely to end in a whole lots of tears, bruises, or embarrassment.

So from that turning point of Easter 1999 I moved forward with an incredible new insight into getting the most out of life. I needed to make better choices and in order to do that I needed to learn what better options were available to me, and then how I could go about making those new options a part of my life. And that is when my life took a completely new course for the better. I had the boat, with a newly refurbished motor attached to the back, filled with the best equipment and essentials I would need along the way, a map and guidebooks to help me navigate the paths ahead, and a new destination. It was called living a life by design. Choosing happiness. Adding more of what worked and getting rid of the excess baggage that no longer served me. Then sharing all that I learned along the way, so that someone following along behind me could get all the benefit of the mistakes I had made and insights I had gained along the way.

The wayward journey from that point in 1999 has seen me visit, travel through and sometimes work in over 50 countries now. I have seen many parts of the globe and met people from numerous cultures that had very little in a material sense, but radiated happiness, vitality and appreciation, and I have met others that seemingly have the 'good life' but lack any real joy and wonder in their lives. I had always been a curious kid and wanted to know 'why' things were the way they were. Why some people where happy and others weren't? Why some people had great health and others struggled through a day. Why some people achieved the goals they set out to achieve and why some don't even know what they want. It is said that curiosity killed the cat. But I say that curiosity adds wonder, excitement and insight to our lives.

Curiosity causes our brains to light up at the prospect of learning something new. So I ask you to be curious as you read this book. Every chapter is an opportunity to learn something new. This book is not called The Rulebook to Happiness; it is called *The Guidebook to Happiness*. I want to guide you to view your internal world and your external world with a new set of eyes, stimulated by that curious and limitless mind of yours.

This book is for anyone who has dreamed of stepping up to a new level, who wants more from this journey called life and themselves, and like me, realizes that we only know what we know. It is time to get the tools, techniques and strategies that will actually cause you to think in a new way, form new empowering habits and therefore cause you to create a new life experience. A leopard may not be able to change its spots, but any person that has the right tools, techniques and strategies, and the desire to use them, is only one step away from an entirely new experience. That new experience could be a whole new life. A life filled with more certainty, with a lightness of spirit, with more excitement and an extra boost of passion. If you are ready for that sort of journey then you have definitely ended up at the right place. Thank you for allowing me to be your guide as you enjoy more than ever before this amazing journey on the way to a remarkable destination of your choosing.

What is
The Guidebook to Happiness?

This book is designed to increase your default level of happiness.

What is this elusive little thing called 'happiness'? What does happiness even mean? I think it is quite different for all of us and unique to all of us. Rather than defining it in fixed or scientific terms, I suggest that 'happiness' is more about something we experience — a by-product of the things we do, rather than something we find. It is more a sense of *being*, rather than the act of walking around with a huge smile on our face (although science does tell us that the act of smiling can change our emotional state for the better).

For some, happiness is related to feeling a deep sense of peace. For others, happiness is a bubbling of love and joy in their heart, enjoying feelings of belonging, or that they really matter. Perhaps for you happiness is knowing you are heading in the right direction as you make your way towards your personal higher purpose. Or maybe you are like me and happiness is a cocktail of all of these things, which in turn causes a cocktail of positive emotions to flow through your body.

Whatever happiness means to you specifically, the purpose of this book is to remind you that you can have more of all the good things and experiences you seek in life. I recall reading many years ago that the original meaning of the word 'pursuit' had more to do with *practicing* than *chasing after*; rewording the common phrase, 'the pursuit of happiness' into 'the practise of happiness'.

This is how I have since come to understand happiness, on my upward, sideward, backward, entirely-off-the-playing-field and onward life journey.

Happiness is not just about what you achieve, it is about what you experience, and who you become along the way.

While I intend on sharing with you the best of what I have learnt over the last 20 years, I also intend on keeping it light and fun.

The Guidebook to Happiness will be INFORMATIVE, INSIGHTFUL, FUN and prompt you to take specific ACTIONS towards your desired life. It is also strategically designed to be short and sweet. I have purposefully chosen not to fill it with scientific research findings, images of activated brain regions in the prefrontal lobe in response to specific thoughts, tabulated scientific data proving why rest is important to you at a physiological and psychological level, or detailed findings from the isolated regions around the world where humans experience the greatest levels of health, happiness and longevity. I have included, however, a comprehensive guide to the books, programs, authors, experts and other sources covered in this book should you seek a deeper level of understanding on any topic.

Having traveled through more than 50 countries over the years I know the life-saving value of a good-quality guidebook. *The Guidebook to Happiness* is designed to be just that — a guidebook to take you in the right direction in life. Refer to it often. Write on it, give it dogs' ears, fold it up, pop it in your back pocket, lend it to your friends, and use it to help you experience a much greater level of happiness. I truly look forward to sharing this next stage of your journey with you.

What to pack: The essentials

Before I dive into sharing the 21 greatest happiness tips and strategies contained herein, let me reiterate the main messages and themes I want you to travel with throughout this book.

Responsibility

Taking personal responsibility is one of the keys to personal development, transformation, increased consciousness and a whole load of other good stuff (to be overly scientific).

Learning to take personal responsibility was a damn big pill for me to swallow — wasn't my life in a mess because of all the 'bad things' happening to me? When I took an honest look at the root cause of those bad things I had to wake up to their being a result of really bad choices I had made. Ouch! It was all me. The moment I became courageous enough to admit that, I was opened up to a world of possibility and transformation.

Not taking personal responsibility for your choices and results in life is like being the Captain of a ship who refuses to steer its course. You will be at the mercy of the elements and could end up in the middle of *Whoknowswhere*. Without personal responsibility you have no control over the bad or the good.

Alternatively, by keeping your hands on the steering wheel you can decide the direction you set sail for, how you face the gale force winds of life and how deeply you enjoy the beautiful moments of calm waters and gentle breezes.

I urge you to consider your life from this moment onwards as belonging to you. You are the Captain of the vessel that will take you through life. You will be in control of which course you take, the speed at which you travel and the amazing destinations you will get to explore. As is often quoted in Neuro Linguistic Programming (NLP), 'all you need is within you now'.

Energy. It is everything ... and it is also everything

While many of us do not have the slightest understanding of how Einstein came up with his famous insight, $E = mc^2$, we do know that the entire universe and everything within it is made up of energy: the book you are reading (or Kindle or tablet); the hand you are holding it with; the chair, floor, sand, grassy knoll, bench, or younger sibling you are currently sitting on. We are all made from energy vibrating at different frequencies. The results we get in life depend on two things in relation to that energy:

1.   How much energy we have (or generate), and

2.   How we direct the energy we have.

If we have very little energy then we are unlikely to be able to create big results. We are unable to make big changes. We are unable to handle life's inevitable challenges as well.

The more energy that we have at our disposal, the greater the results we can create and the less affected we are by the winds that blow against our sail — it's like having a powerful inbuilt motor ready to use on our sail boat, if needed.

Alternatively, it is no good having that extra energy or motor on our boat if we steer it towards a hidden reef or ride it across the waves making us more likely to capsize. We need to point that energy in the right direction, so we get to our desired destination — the one with coconut trees, sunshine, soft sand, a hammock; I am sure you see the picture. It is not only about the size of the motor or the amount of energy it can deliver, it is also about where and how we direct that energy to get the best results.

My aim is to help you develop higher levels of energy and then help you determine the best strategies to use and places to focus that energy so you get the best possible results.

At a very practical level, over the course of this book I give you specific

Happiness Strategies to increase your physical energy. I will also teach you how to have more mental energy by increasing your vibrational energy, that is, your vitality and mental functioning, and help you reduce the amount of energy you waste through ineffective thinking, limiting beliefs and draining behaviors.

I will help you become your absolute *Best Self.* I will help you tap into more of your unlimited potential and expand your mental and emotional consciousness to a whole new level. I guarantee that if you open yourself to new ways of understanding and perceiving the world around you and APPLY the strategies I suggest in this guidebook to happiness, your life will become the greatest adventure you ever could have imagined: 'Hoorah!!!'

My passion in life and quest for now and the next 62 years (which will take me up to 105 years of age and my current target) is to help you fully express your uniqueness and potential and become the best you can be. In order to do that I offer you 21 ridiculously simple insights and life lessons that have been the result of a lot of my blood, sweat and tears (plus a lot of laughter, joy, wonder and amazement) and echoed by many inspiring thought-leaders through the ages. You also have access to some great resources and freebies to help you stay the happiness course, which you will find at *www.theguidebooktohappiness.com* in the 'Bonuses for Book Owners' tab. I have even created a Personal Journal for you, plus a mini happiness course you will have access to! You will be sent weekly activities and training from me based on the most effective Happiness Strategies. If you follow them, you will create some strong momentum and become unstoppable in the face of the most raging storms and gale force winds.

How to use this guidebook

Just like a good-quality travel guidebook, *The Guidebook to Happiness* is about helping you work out the best 'Things to Do', how to avoid 'Dangers and Annoyances', and 'Getting There' when it comes to happiness. In this guidebook you will learn what to do, what not to do and what to keep doing.

You can work your way through chronologically, or you can jump from chapter to chapter if that is what you prefer. However, I encourage you to read Chapter 1 first as this deals with the mind, which is ground zero when it comes to getting results in your life. As Roman Stoic philosopher Seneca said, 'Everything hangs on one's thinking.'

To help you make better choices, each chapter finishes with a Summary and a list of simple Happiness Strategies to undertake so you can start making positive changes in your life today. If you would like to delve deeper into a particular topic there is a list of reference material at the end of the book.

Below is a quick guide to finding specific topics if you have a particular destination in mind.

Desired Destination	Recommended Chapters
Increased energy levels	All
Reduced stress	All (especially 3, 5–9, 13, 15–18)
Improved relationships	1–3, 7, 8, 10, 13, 16–18
Increased health	1, 3, 9, 12, 14, 15
Less affected by others	1, 3, 7, 8, 10, 14, 16–18, 21
Increased productivity	1, 2, 5, 6, 11, 12, 15, 21
Increased clarity	1-3, 6, 8, 13, 16, 17, 20
Increased peace and calm	1, 3, 5, 6–9, 12, 13, 15, 17, 21

Snapshot:
How happy am I right now?

What you don't measure you don't notice. With that in mind, before we get started, I have a quick exercise for you to do that has proven insightful for numerous clients and me over the years.

As a participant in a 4-day personal development seminar several years ago, I was asked to write down my values on Day 1. When I reviewed them on Day 4, one particular value stood out — I could not believe I had once held this value, and only four days prior. If it had not been written in my notebook, in my handwriting, with my pen, I would not have believed that I could change so much in four days. So I challenge you to measure your levels of happiness today, as you start *The Guidebook to Happiness*, and then do so again when you reach the end. You might just surprise yourself with your growth over such a short period of time.

Obviously if you speed-read the book in a few hours and don't apply any of the Happiness Strategies you are unlikely to change, but who knows; maybe one idea will lodge in your mind and open up a whole new realm of possibility.

On the following table record in the 'Start' column your current levels of happiness in key areas of your life. When you have finished the book and implemented the strategies within it, fill in the 'End' column to measure your progress. (A copy of the table is in *The Guidebook to Happiness Personal Journal*. To download the Personal Journal plus other free goodies go to the 'Bonuses for Book Owners' tab at *www.theguidebooktohappiness.com*.)

Here's to onwards and upwards as your consciousness expands to new heights!

Categories	NUMBER 1	NUMBER 10	Start	End
Daily Joy	I dread my days.	I can't wipe the ridiculously huge smile off my face.		
Optimism	Life is there to break me.	I have complete trust and faith in life to give me everything I ask for.		
Gratitude	I am not really grateful for anything.	I am so grateful for the life I have and everything in it. I say 'thank you' to life/the universe ALL the time.		
Enthusiasm	I hate anything new or different and I am not interested in trying.	I love life, love its changes, can't wait to experience more. I'm jumping out of my skin.		

Categories	NUMBER 1	NUMBER 10	Start	End
Passion	I have no idea what it even means.	I feel vibrant energy coming from my core that overflows into everything that I do.		
Energy Level	I have no energy.	It is ridiculously high. I could power a small village off my excess energy.		
Consciousness/ Self-Awareness	I feel like a hamster on a spinning wheel. Knee-jerk reactions rule.	I own 100% of my thoughts, actions and results and can change them as required.		
Purpose	I have no clue, no plan and no interest.	I have a definite plan on how to live my highest purpose and achieve ALL my goals.		

Categories	Where a number 1 would be...	And a number 10 would be...	Start	End
Knowledge & Wisdom	I don't know why I feel, act or behave the way I do. I am clueless.	I have a deep understanding of how the mind and body are integrated and how I can get results.		
Self Love	I hate myself. I consciously/sub-consciously hurt myself.	I have deep love, approval and respect for myself. I don't need external approval at all.		
Integrity	I am totally out of alignment with integrity and often lie to myself and others.	I am 100% honest with myself and others regardless of the consequences.		
Sense Of Happiness	I am unhappy. I am not enjoying life. Life sucks!	I love my life. I love the planet and everyone in it. I love myself.		

CHAPTER 1:

It all starts in the mind

Human beings can alter their lives by altering their attitudes of mind.
William James, American psychologist and philosopher

When I first started working on a book about increasing our default level of happiness I came up with the concept of exercising our happiness muscles in the world's biggest gym. The world's biggest gym is our life experience and the world around us, the place in which we conduct our workouts in every waking moment. The *world's biggest gym* is also within our own mind — in our mind is where our entire life experience is processed and stored, and our future life created. Earl Nightingale, American motivational speaker and author, made famous the phrase, 'We become what we think.' Marcus Aurelius, in addition to being a main character in the movie *Gladiator*, was a philosopher and in his spare time, the Emperor of Rome. He said, 'Our life is what our thoughts make it.' Ralph Waldo Emerson said, 'The ancestor of every action is a thought.' Buddha said, 'Our life is shaped by our mind; we become what we think.' And the list goes on. So we might be onto something here when we say that the world's biggest gym is in fact in each of our minds. It's the perfect place to start this happiness guidebook.

I generally use the term 'mind' rather than 'brain' throughout this book. While the brain is that grey, funny-looking organ in the upper posterior of the cranium that weighs about 2% of our overall body weight, the 'mind' is the result of the brain at work. The mind is the power that is able to create captivating works of art, design tall skyscrapers, build huge bridges, write beautiful poetry, define ideals that inspire nations and move figurative mountains. Neuroscience tells us that our brain continues to produce brain cells (neurons) throughout our whole life and that our mental facilities are not fixed, but are like plastic in our hands. The more we use our mind the greater it becomes, from a functional perspective and even a physical one.

While we've established the fact that the brain is the most important tool in the human body and the mind can create for us the ultimate human experience, I want to dig a little deeper. Allow me to unveil *Mind Mechanics 101: The inner workings of your extraordinarily powerful human mind*. Get ready to be amazed, intrigued and changed forever.

Cellular biologist, Dr Bruce Lipton, in his book *The Biology of Belief* suggests that the number of environmental stimuli the conscious mind can interpret per second is about 40; compare this to the power of the subconscious mind, which can interpret about 20 million. Yes, you read that right: 20 million! Contemplate the huge difference between what the conscious mind is handling each second, and what the subconscious mind is pumping out in that same second: the subconscious mind is about 500,000 times more powerful than the conscious mind and is therefore a mighty ally in the expression of our greatness and full potential.

The subconscious mind can also take in the entire external picture of what we are looking at, including the sounds, smells and physical sensations, in one sweeping motion, as opposed to the conscious mind, which is limited to seeing only that which we consciously focus our attention on. You might not have noticed that red car in the distance, sitting on the edge of your peripheral vision, but your subconscious mind did. The subconscious mind can detect sounds that are much lower in frequency and volume than you can consciously hear. This means it can detect sounds (and even conversations) that are taking place at a great distance. Your subconscious mind is hearing all the conversations in a room, not just the ones that you decide to consciously listen to. And there is mounting scientific evidence to support the idea that the subconscious mind can interpret signals at a vibrational level, which can travel to and from a much greater distance than any of our conscious sensing is able to reach.

This would explain things we have all experienced before, such as thinking about a person and then suddenly hearing from them a short time later when we've not had contact with them for months. When this happens once it might be a coincidence. But when this happens several times, with many different people, then we need to understand that there is a lot more happening than meets our conscious eye and current understanding.

In essence, your subconscious mind is taking in the whole picture, hearing the whole show and picking up signals or impulses that you can't consciously detect. If I were a child at the playground deciding who I wanted on my team, my good friend Sub Conscious would definitely be my first choice.

I am sure you are starting to see a pattern here — the subconscious mind is extremely powerful and incredibly intelligent. But here are a couple of other things that you may not have fully realized before now: The subconscious mind does not judge right or wrong. My subconscious mind (unfortunately) does not say to me, 'That is a really stupid idea Carl and I think it would be best if you did not play out that thought, because it might end up with your partner leaving you and your health being ruined.' Instead the subconscious mind asks, 'Exactly when would you like that new (highly stressful and 100 hour per week) work opportunity to start?' The subconscious mind is in the game of *delivering*. It is there to make stuff happen — for better or worse.

Essentially, the subconscious mind determines what we (our conscious self) want by *observing the images that we play in our mind and noting the level of emotional intensity that accompanies them*. It figures that if we are playing the same movie over and over again, in addition to expressing a high level of emotional intensity, then we must passionately want whatever is in our mind.

Have you ever played a movie in your mind of something that you really really *did not want* to happen and felt strong emotional intensity (anxiety) along with it? It is not surprising then that it led to a place affectionately known as 'Getting what you DID NOT WANT'!

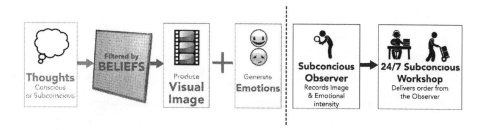

I have created the diagram above to show you how the conscious mind communicates with the subconscious powerhouse, or what I like to call our *24/7 Subconscious Workshop*.

The clearer you make the image in your mind, the easier it is for your 24/7 Subconscious Workshop to deliver the end result. In the diagram the Subconscious Observer is watching the movie you are creating and playing in the cinema of your mind. The clearer it is for the observer to see what you want, the quicker and easier it is for the subconscious workshop to start the creation process. I personally believe that the more clear a picture is in your mind — that is, the colours are bright and clear, the contrast is high and the focus is sharp — the closer you are to attaining your goal.

The subconscious mind is amazing, but after all, nothing is designed to be perfect all the time. So here is the catch. Unfortunately, our friend Sub Conscious cannot read letters and especially cannot understand the words 'I do not want...'. The subconscious mind is all about the PICTURE you have playing in your conscious mind and its accompanying level of emotional intensity. Remember, it figures the more emotional energy that you attach to the picture, be it excitement or pure anxiety, the more you must want it.

Let us conduct a very simple exercise to highlight what happens when we think in terms of 'I do not want'. Please create a picture now of the thought, 'I do not want an elephant'. What does your picture look like? Does it involve a large grey animal with four legs, a trunk and big floppy ears by any chance? The subconscious mind has not understood the words 'I do not want'; it has only seen the elephant we've thought about.

The soundtrack feature of the movie in our mind also allows us to embellish the images to our heart's content. You can add the sound of a large audience giving you a thunderous standing ovation after you dazzled them with your dancing performance, or the echo of fireworks can resound off the distant mountains as you passionately kiss, Hollywood style, that person you have been dreamily watching from afar for 7 years. But it pays no attention to your voice in the background narrating what you want to happen. It is like shouting over the picture of the elephant, 'Just so you know, I do not want an elephant!' The mind sees the elephant regardless of your words.

I often say to my clients, in life we don't get what we WANT, we don't get what we NEED, we actually get what we EXPECT; so often, that is the picture that we are playing on loop in our mind and the emotions that we are turning on in our bodies. For instance, you might expect a meeting at work to go poorly, so you play the picture in your mind of the meeting turning into a disaster, ending with no resolution, contracts being canceled and relationships adversely affected. You link your emotional anxiety to the picture for effect. So your subconscious mind actually believes that you want the meeting to go poorly and is already well practised in how to feel anxiety. During the meeting, to which you've arrived late, your mind is all over the place — you cannot focus, you make inappropriate comments, you are easily distracted, you offend the other people and it may very well end up as you 'expected' it to. You are even anxious for no reason. Was it a result of something external, or was your subconscious mind 'helping' you get the result it thought you wanted? EXPECT the best and focus the incredible power of your mind on the ideal image of what result you want and it will get to work 24/7 to bring you just the result you are after!

Let me also explain the difference between fantasizing and visualization at this point. Fantasizing is just letting images float dreamily through your mind. Visualization is similar to this but is consciously focusing the mind, making it more specific in detail, accompanied by very specific feelings, and repeated systematically. In sporting visualization, it is most effective to visualize not only winning the race, but also overcoming all of the challenges along the way. For a 100m sprint athlete it would be like seeing a perfect start, an explosive first 10m, a build up over the next 60m and then an extra burst of speed for the last 30m, to finally win the race in record time and feeling the elevated emotions of having won the race.

Now we know how the subconscious mind works, we can develop a system to get the absolute most out of it. And the system we can use is simple. In fact, very young children have been mastering it for years! How many young children do you know who picture what they *don't* want for Christmas or their birthday? Children are generally masters of picturing what they do want and experiencing the positive emotions of playing with their new toy. And that is the secret key to success. To get the very most out of our subconscious mind we need to create visions, pictures and movies in our conscious mind of all the things that WE REALLY WANT in our lives; and then, just like a child does, feel excitement course through our bodies as if we have already achieved the end result.

People often ask how to remove the negative thoughts or pictures from their minds. Have you ever walked into a dark room? How do you remove the darkness that has taken up residence there? You turn on the light. It is that simple. To remove the dark you bring in the light. It is the same with your mind. To remove the bad thoughts or pictures, you just fill your mind with good pictures. Introduce pictures of the things you want: pictures of the relationships you want to experience, of the abundance you want to experience. If you fill your mind with all of these desired pictures there is little room, if any, left for the 'bad' stuff to take up residence in your mind.

The subconscious mind is greatly influenced by the emotional intensity that we attach to the movies in our mind — it is almost like there is a meter that measures the emotional intensity of our movie as we play it. Our 24/7 subconscious workshop begins creating the physical reality of the images based on the level of emotional intensity accompanying them. The higher the emotional intensity, the higher the priority to get the job done. Again the subconscious mind does not determine 'good' or 'bad' goals, it just works on the ones it thinks are most important, based on the emotional intensity you feel.

Do you feel you have a better understanding of the difference between the conscious and subconscious minds and how they work together? The neocortex is the most developed part of the human brain and it allows us to create the pictures that we want, even to create images of things that have not happened yet — to dream up anything we want. It is up to us to create in our minds the most inspiring, empowering and enjoyable images we can, thus giving our subconscious mind very clear directions on exactly what we want.

What you will generally find is that when you have a goal in mind, it will start off a little unclear; but over time, if you keep focusing on it, keep working on it, it will get clearer and clearer. When it is 'crystal' clear then it is only moments away from being in your life. It is a done deal. If you can see a picture of what you want in your mind then it is possible to bring it into physical form. Walt Disney called this *Imagineering*! And Albert Einstein said, 'Our imagination is our most powerful attribute.' Everything that has ever been made by humans is created twice. First in someone's mind and then in the physical form. It all starts by us utilizing the amazing creative power of the human mind.

One last reminder of what it means to 'visualize' a crystal clear picture. When I talk about visualizing I am not only talking about the silent movie picture in your mind. Just like with modern movies, there is a soundtrack, feelings associated with the movie and an entire sensory experience. The more you can visualize the complete picture, with sounds, smells, taste and touch, the more you make it real. So visualizing is not just about the picture. It is about bringing a picture in your mind to life.

This chapter is at the very front of *The Guidebook to Happiness* because it is such a crucial element in your success. Like I said at the start, the world's biggest gym is actually in your mind. That is where your world, your reality, your successes and your setbacks are created. When you master your mind you shape your destiny. So here's to creating and crafting a beautiful mind that is filled with all the wonderful things you want in life, leaving no space for the things you don't want. When you truly integrate the power of your conscious and subconscious mind you actually become the person who is able to achieve the picture you hold in your mind. You are abuzz with the power of creation. You now are creating your own destiny and strengthening your happiness muscles.

Summary

1. Remove the phrase 'I do not want...' from your vocabulary. It only leads you to imagine what you don't want.

2. Always use the phrase 'I want...'. This way, your mind is already focusing on creating your dreams.

3. Make the images of what you want as clear as you possibly can. Add lots of colors, sounds and even textures, smells and tastes. Recreate the picture in your mind as if it is really happening and experience all of the emotions that go with it as well. Be the Creative Director of your own life.

4. Get emotionally engaged with what you really want when you are forming the picture in your mind. When you start forming strong emotions, you are setting up a chemical process in your body, which actually causes you to physically take action. Without emotion our body will stay in the one place.

5. To remove recurring negative thoughts, pictures or images, have positive replacements ready to swap them with as soon as they pop up in your consciousness. Remember the question, 'How do you remove the darkness from a room?' The simple answer is, 'You turn on the light.' You don't have to 'remove' negative thoughts; you just need to crowd them out with your enlightened new thoughts. Practise makes perfect when it comes to creating visual images of the things you want in your life.

Happiness Strategies

1. What is one important goal that you have in your life right now? Pause for 2 minutes to write this down now, or jot down a time to do so in your diary. When you have written down your goal, set aside a time at least once a day for the next 30 days to practice visualizing your life with the goal already achieved. How does it feel to have reached it? Get all of your senses involved in the mental movie you make and get as emotionally engaged as possible. Visualizing is like a muscle. The more you use it, the stronger it will get.

2. Over the next 30 days, catch yourself out if you use the words 'I DO NOT WANT'. Practise quickly replacing it with the image of what you DO WANT in your life. If you are having any problems with this, ask the nearest 6-year-old to help out.

CHAPTER 2:

Half the equation in the science of happiness

If you want to be happy, set a goal that commands your thoughts, liberates your energy, and inspires your hopes.
Andrew Carnegie, Scottish-American industrialist and philanthropist

Another great book on happiness — aside from *The Guidebook to Happiness* of course — is *Happier* by Tal Ben-Shahar. Tal Ben-Shahar is a philosophy and positive psychology professor and lecturer at Harvard University and a leading authority on the science and study of happiness. He suggests a simple yet rather profound principle — for happiness to exist in our lives we need to experience *current pleasure* and *future meaning* in our lives. Let's put pleasure to the side for now (sorry) and focus on future meaning for our happiness.

When our lives have a positive meaning we tend to jump out of bed in the morning at a ridiculously early hour, excited and expectant about the day, because we know today is going to bring us a few steps closer to that which holds great meaning for us. Aristotle tells us, 'Man is a goal-seeking animal. His life only has meaning if he is reaching out and striving for his goals.'

Having goals and moving in the direction of those goals is absolutely essential for your happiness. If you do not have any defined goals then you are likely to have less tangible meaning in your life and may even feel a little bit lost or without direction. Have you ever felt truly lost in your life? Like when you went for a walk in a forest or a new city and had no idea where you were? How did getting lost make you feel? Anxious? Scared? Panicked? Having no goals in your life may not seem like a big deal, but below the surface it can lead you to experience the same emotions as when you were lost in that forest.

In order to give your life true meaning and to experience more happiness in your life, it is extremely important to have a clear vision of what you want. The more 'worthy' your goals, the more meaning you are likely to derive from them. It was Earl Nightingale who said, 'Success is the progressive realization of a worthy goal.' That means you can actually start feeling successful and happy as you are moving in the direction of a goal you've deemed worthy.

Now the subject of setting and attaining goals can fill a book by itself, so in order to provide you the best, most essential information, below I have provided a comprehensive list of the key points when it comes to goal setting. These insights are based on the latest research and my 20 years of experience as an expert planner and strategist.

The key points on becoming an ELITE Goal Setter:

1. Take the time to figure out what your purpose in life might be. The more inspiring it is, the more you will be drawn along. See if you can find or define something of greater meaning in your life. A great purpose is one that is good for you, good for others and good for the greater good. Your purpose does not have to be to change the planet or save humanity. Mother Teresa did not set out to alleviate the poverty of the whole world; she set as her purpose to alleviate the poverty in Calcutta and it grew from there. If it has not yet come to you, just plant the question in the back of your mind. Don't try and force it, but let it come. It will come when you are ready.

2. Now set a long-term goal which will allow you to fully express the purpose in your life and add to it richness and deeper meaning. Then develop medium-term and short-term goals to support your long-term goal. The

aim is to align all your goals. If you achieve your short-term goal it brings you closer to your medium-term goal which brings you closer to your longer-term goal and ultimately, it all brings you closer to expressing and living by your higher purpose in life. This is called 'vertical coherence'. US Psychologists Sheldon and Kasser found that people who are mentally healthy and happy have a higher degree of vertical coherence in their goals.

3. Once you are clear about your goals it is easier to make decisions about other opportunities that come up. If an opportunity comes to you that does not support your goals and does not warrant changing your current goals then reject the opportunity (or distraction).

4. Set your priorities and root them in what matters most. Dr Heidi Halvorson, social psychologist, author of the book *Succeed,* and one of the foremost researchers on setting goals, writes:

    > The researchers found that if any of the three extrinsic aspirations — for money, fame, or beauty — was very high for an individual relative to the three intrinsic aspirations — meaningful relationships, personal growth, and community contributions — the individual was also more likely to display poorer mental health. For example, having an unusually strong aspiration for material success was associated with narcissism, anxiety, depression, and poorer social functioning as rated by a trained clinical psychologist.

    It is ok for your health and happiness to want money if it is the *by-product* of doing something else more meaningful, as opposed to being the goal itself.

5. Always write down your goals. Again, the findings of social psychologists' research suggests that the probability of attaining your goals increases by up to 400% if you physically write down your goals. I recommend putting pen to paper to record your goals, as opposed to tapping them out on your keyboard and hitting the print button — that feels a little bit too much like cheating, and your goals deserve better. (Note: the experiment was based on writing on a piece of paper rather than typing on a computer.)

6. Make sure your goals are worth what it will take to achieve them. If you are likely to lose or suffer diminished relationships with your partner, friends, children, social life and leisure time in the process of achieving your major goal, it might be time to come up with a new goal or set one that's a little less demanding.

7. Make sure that achieving your goal depends solely on you. If you set a goal that is dependent on the government changing, or the government abolishing personal income tax for those that earn less than $250,000 per year, or a set of lotto numbers coming out in a certain sequence, then you might be the proud recipient of a goal that never happens and a pillow full of tears. Set goals the outcomes of which you can control by your efforts, your research, your decisions, your superior knowledge and your awesome tenacity.

8. Something I did not realize until I delved more deeply into researching the psychology of setting goals is that if a person believes that their goal is achievable and also easy to attain, they are LESS LIKELY to achieve their goal than someone that believes that their goal is achievable, but *difficult* to attain. If you know that your goal is going to be hard to achieve you are more prepared for the inevitable obstacles and setbacks; and therefore more likely to succeed.

9. The clearer your goal is articulated both on paper and in your mind, the more likely you are to achieve that goal. When you write down your goal ensure that it is crystal clear. Write it as though you are going to hand your goal statement to a third-party contractor (aka your subconscious mind) who will make or manifest it for you. If it is not clear you are unlikely to get what you want, when you want it. If you have a goal to travel to South America to walk the Inca Trail, but do not write down a date, then the trip may not happen for another 25 years. If the directions aren't clear then the delivery will not be either.

10. I have saved the best and most important point for last. Setting and attaining goals is more about who you become, or have to become, along the way

to achieving your goal. If you want to achieve a goal at a higher level than what you have achieved in the past, you need to become more than you were in the past. You need to think and act differently. That is what we are working on throughout the rest of this *Guidebook* — helping you step up to a new level of being and therefore a new level of achieving. New you + new thinking and acting = new RESULTS!!

Happiness Strategies

1. Work on defining your purpose or higher meaning in life. Your purpose does not need to be too specific, but more of a guiding philosophy and theme for your life.

2. Write down your Top 10 Goals in Life. Even if you put no science or strategy into the attainment of these goals, just by writing them down you have increased the likelihood of attaining them by up to 400%.

3. Do a Goal Setting course. I highly recommend either the WorldsBIGGESTGym™ *Become an ELITE Goal Setter* workshop or the *30-Day Happiness Challenge*. Brian Tracy, a renowned business and success coach and entrepreneur, also conducts some great goal-setting programs. Past participants have suggested that learning how to set goals was more valuable to them than their 4-year university degree. Setting goals is definitely one essential KEY to being happier in life.

As a special bonus, I have included the 6-Step strategy to *Become an ELITE Goal Setter* in the Bonuses for Book Owners tab at *www.theguidebooktohappiness. com* or if you are like me and want to understand more of the 'why' behind the strategy you might also like to check out my (mini) digital book called *Become an ELITE Goal Setter* at Amazon.

CHAPTER 3:

Down which path are your beliefs taking you?

If you believe you can, or believe you can't, you are correct.
Henry Ford, industrialist, innovator, once one of the world's wealthiest people

'Do I believe that I can write the perfect chapter or am I immobilized by the thought that I may not do this (huge) topic justice?' That is one of the thoughts that popped into my head as I opened up a blank document on my computer and readied my (two) typing fingers. As Henry Ford articulated so eloquently, the end result is less about what is external to us and more about what is going on inside us, and in particular in the grey matter between our ears. Beliefs are one of the key aspects that shape our lives and determine the outcomes for us in any given situation. Your beliefs are either supporting you magically on your journey through life, or they are turning your path into a sea of mud 2-foot deep. Beliefs are the software that drives your subconscious habits and the filter for all of your thoughts. Since they are such a powerful tool it is essential that we learn more about them, so we can activate their creative power for our vitality, health, happiness and on-going success.

The subject of beliefs really is broad, so this chapter will only scratch the surface. Here, I focus on what beliefs are and how we can use them to empower our lives and the results we see from them. (For a lot more detail, read Dr Bruce Lipton's book *The Biology of Belief;* alternatively you can get a copy of my eBook

'*Your Beliefs are Controlling Your Life*' at *www.theguidebooktohappiness. com*.) Dealing with beliefs, in particular disempowering beliefs, is a big part of the work I do as a Life Coach. We are walking on transformative ground when we talk about beliefs. At the time of writing this, I was listening to an interview between Darren Hardy, publisher of SUCCESS Magazine, and Jermaine Paul, winner of the second series of *The Voice* (USA). When Jermaine was asked about the turning point in his career he said that it was when he started to believe in himself: His success came when he changed his beliefs about his own worth, ability and potential. Beliefs are powerful stuff.

Before I start calling you Alice and taking you down any rabbit holes, let us first agree on what a belief is. The Oxford Dictionary (online) tells us a belief is 'an acceptance that something exists or is true, especially one without proof'. I don't know about you, but that definition gives me the distinct impression that 'beliefs' are sort of like play dough in your hands — especially the words 'without proof'. And acceptance from whom? Us? Society? The President, Prime Minister or Queen? This is the first point and it is absolutely profound: When you come to the understanding that beliefs are not laws of nature, or laws that govern the universe, you start to understand that they might be a tool that you can use to your best advantage. Some of the happiest people I have met or worked with are those with the most flexible beliefs, and the greatest openness to explore alternatives to their beliefs.

So if beliefs may or may not be true and may be held with or without proof, where the heck do they come from? I am glad you asked! There are two main ways that our beliefs are formed: genetically; and through the external environment of our earliest years.

After a lot of research, speculation and calculation it is suggested that the amount of genetic programming we inherit is about 50%. Whether the case for each individual is plus or minus a few percent either side of 50, there is still plenty of opportunity left for us to create our own destiny. So if our mother or father had a strong belief that the world was an unsafe place and behaved in a fearful manner to support that belief, there is a chance their belief and behavior may be genetically passed on. Before we put the lid on the excuse of 'So sorry but I got this from my parents', I also want to point out that the study of epigenetics suggests that we have the ability to change the expression of our genes. Dr Joe Dispenza, author of *Evolve Your Brain*, also suggests that we only use about 1.5% of the genes in our DNA anyway. So while genetics and DNA have an impact on the formation of our core beliefs, they are not as fixed as was once thought.

The more obvious way we form our beliefs is from the people that are in our lives in our early childhood, especially up until about 7 years of age. We tend to form the same beliefs as the people that are most influential in our lives, such as our parents or primary carers. The reason why we sponge up their beliefs (whether they are right, wrong, good or bad) is that our brains are still developing and in a theta brainwave state. Why is that interesting? Well hypnosis is best performed when a patient is in a theta brainwave state, otherwise known as a *suggestive state*. As young children we do not have the ability to filter out the beliefs we are being taught (verbally or visually observed) and that is why sometimes our beliefs make absolutely no sense at all. We took them in word-for-word and literally.

Once we learn these beliefs, that *may or may not be true*, we start to live by them in our own lives. We actually start to become our beliefs. Believing 'I am worthless' is the result of being told 'you are worthless'; 'it is hard for someone of my ethnicity/culture/stature/demographic to be successful' is what you were taught as truth. 'I have to put everyone first' came from being told or taught by example that 'you have to put everyone first'. The more we play these beliefs out, the more the body memorizes the way we have to behave to sustain those beliefs (based on what we were told or saw played out), and the more our beliefs become subconscious, making us completely unaware of them. Both Dr Bruce Lipton and Dr Joe Dispenza suggest that 95% of the time, we are operating on subconscious programs and beliefs.

Before I talk about how we can use this information to increase our happiness, health, vitality and even success, let me reiterate that our beliefs are not necessarily true. That is, they are not true in 100% of cases, 100% of the time. They were picked up at a young age, very literally, when we had no ability to filter them or say 'that sounds like a ridiculously stupid idea and I am not sure holding that belief will serve me well for the rest of my life'. Our genetics or DNA does not trap us to a fixed outcome. Beliefs determine our behavior (or actions), which leads to a particular result. And most of our beliefs and the behavior they cause are subconscious.

So here is the great news. Just as we learned and practiced our beliefs, so too can we unlearn and 'unpractice' them. Figuring out which beliefs are EMPOWERING and which are DISEMPOWERING will lead to, you guessed it, the path to happiness, which requires a lot less of the disempowering stuff and a lot more of the empowering stuff. We can even take it one step further by replacing the disempowering beliefs with empowering beliefs.

Empowering beliefs are the beliefs, statements or affirmations that we tell ourselves, which lead us to feel confident, energized, inspired, creative, connected, loved, powerful, courageous, and the like. Disempowering beliefs make us feel fearful, disconnected, worried, inferior, unloved, uninspired, reactive (instead of creative) and a host of other negative feelings. It is not so much about whether our beliefs are 'right' or 'wrong', it is about how they make us feel. When we feel great we are more likely to do great, and when we feel like crap we are more likely to perform below our level of capability. Our health is greatly affected by the number of positive emotions we experience compared to negative emotions.

Therefore one of the keys to happiness is to work on removing as many disempowering beliefs as possible and replacing them with empowering beliefs. Unfortunately many of us (myself included) have been playing the wrong tune for decades, which means that there can actually be a neural network in the brain; let's call it the 'I cannot experience real happiness in my life because

I am not worthy which I was told as a child' network. The good news from those marvellous neuroscientists and neuropsychologists (in particular Donald Hebb) is that neurons that fire together wire together. Repeating empowering beliefs strengthens their expression and actually causes the brain to change. Alternatively, neurons that don't fire together (or belief statements that we choose to stop repeating because they are disempowering) do not wire together or atrophy in the brain. Yes, we can change our beliefs; yes, it does require effort to make the change.

In the Happiness Strategies below I describe the best way to change beliefs. You have already done it before with Santa Clause, the Easter Bunny, and the belief that your parents knew what they were doing (as opposed to the reality that everyone makes up a lot on the fly and does the best they can with the resources and knowledge they have). There are numerous other ways to work on changing beliefs, such as Neuro Linguistics Programming (NLP), hypnosis, Time Line Therapy, and the LifeLine Technique™, just to name a few. So if you feel yourself getting stuck, seek out some external perspective and assistance.

Summary

1. According to the Oxford Dictionary (online), a belief is 'an acceptance that something exists or is true, especially one without proof'. A belief is not a universal law, like gravity, but is something we have convinced ourselves is true. It can be changed.

2. Our beliefs may not even be our own, but those imparted to us during the suggestive theta brainwave state when we were under 7 years of age.

3. The beliefs that other people taught us may or may not be right. They may be useful or useless. We might have picked up some great stuff along the way, as well as some duds. For instance, if you have a belief right now that you are not enough, or not good enough, or others are more talented than you, then you have been told a little white lie. You are enough. You are

good enough. You have the ability to improve anything that you focus on. All you need is within you now. We are all created equal. It is what we do with that equal-ness that makes the difference.

4. We are not victims of our genes. A lot of research now suggests that our environment can change the expression of our genes. It seems that rather than being a one-way street from our DNA to what we become in life, what we consciously become (and the lifestyle choices we make) can actually change how our DNA plays out. For more information, check out the field of epigenetics or read the work of Dr Bruce Lipton, Dr Joe Dispenza, Dr Candace Pert, and Dr Darren Weissman.

5. Our beliefs cause us to behave in a certain way, often so repeatedly that we are not aware of it. The way we behave determines the results we get in life. If we change our beliefs for the better, we change our results for the better. That is why this topic is SO important.

6. It is not about right or wrong beliefs. The important thing is to determine which beliefs or statements you repetitively say are empowering and which are disempowering. The aim is to tap into more of the empowering beliefs and replace disempowering beliefs with even more empowering beliefs.

7. It is possible to change very strongly held beliefs — think Santa Clause, the Easter Bunny or the Tooth Fairy or 'Mum is always right'. However, it does require energy, effort and persistence to reform to a new way of thinking and behaving.

Happiness Strategies

This has the potential to be a HUGE LIFE-CHANGER if you follow through on it. I find the biggest shift is possible if we swap the most disempowering belief for an empowering belief.

1. Become aware of your thoughts. What are you saying to yourself and how does it make you feel? Tick the feel-good thoughts. Do this for a week.

Choose to take the approach of excitement, rather than disappointment in what you find. Have a laugh at some of the monkey chatter and mad thoughts that pop up in your mind uninvited. A great happiness strategy in itself is to not take ourselves too seriously.

2. Write down the thoughts that make you feel bad. I ask my clients 'where do you feel the most pain, discomfort or challenge in your life?' because I know that generally mixed in amongst that pain is a disempowering belief. What are your most disempowering beliefs?

3. Select which one of the disempowering beliefs you most want to rid and write it down.

4. Now write the exact opposite of that belief. For example, if it is 'I am not worthy'; then write down 'I am worthy'. If it is 'I cannot do it'; write down 'I can do it'.

5. You now know the mantra you will be repeating on a loop recording. Remember that neurons (in the brain) that fire together wire together. Your empowering belief will form a new neural network if you repeat it often enough. Also, to make the process even quicker and more effective, engage the emotions. This way the brain and the body remember who the new you is: the you with empowering beliefs.

6. If you get stuck or feel that you are not sure what to focus on, then you might want to check out the WorldsBIGGESTGym™ *30-Day Happiness Challenge*. Alternatively, track down a good therapist or coach to help you out. You are not alone and do not have to figure all this out by yourself.

CHAPTER 4:

That Newton dude was on to something: What we give out, we get back

Money is a result, wealth is a result, health is a result, illness is a result, your weight is a result. We live in a world of cause and effect.
T Harv Eker, American author, businessman and motivational speaker

Have you ever heard 'insanity' defined as doing the same thing over and over again and expecting a different result each time? I am sure you have, or have at least intuitively known this all along. It would be like adding 1+2+3+4 and hoping to get a different answer than 10 each time. 'What? Not 10 again!' That would be *ludicrous* (which is such an apt word, because it actually sounds silly!). How would you describe using the same thinking you have always used and waiting for your life to miraculously change?

So many of us continue to do things in the same way but keep expecting a different result. That is insane. It was Albert Einstein who famously said, 'We can't solve problems by using the same kind of thinking we used when we created them.' Since we (you and me) are in the business of solving problems and coming up with strategies to enhance the quality of our lives, this is quite a big light bulb moment. Essentially, the message is: we need to change our thinking if we want to obtain different — that is, better — results in life. And that is exactly what *The Guidebook to Happiness* is all about. I am here to work with you to change your thinking and your conscious behaviors so you achieve new and improved results in your life and experience higher levels of happiness.

For this lesson let's introduce the famous Mr Newton. Apparently there is some speculation on the internet as to his full name. Some claim it was 'Lawrence Isaac Newton James'; in any case, I am going with 'Isaac Newton', to which 'Sir' was later added to acknowledge his contribution to physics. And to physics is where I want to turn right now. Sir Isaac Newton's most memorable Law is:

For every action there is an equal and opposite reaction.

As you will note (warning: Australian sarcasm to follow), Newton did not write his *Third Law of Motion* thus:

For a whole bunch of actions, but not all of them, just the ones that make your life easier, there are equal, or sometimes unequal, reactions and sometimes, but not always, opposite reactions.

There is no skirting around the Law on this one. It works whether you believe it or not. It is also known as the *Law of Cause and Effect* and Thomas Edison is quoted as having called it the *Law of Laws*. A lot of Eastern cultures refer to it as the *Law of Karma*, suggesting that what you give out you get back in equal measure. The fact remains that even if you stick your head in the sand, or live your life unconsciously, the law of cause and effect will still play out in your life.

So we need to embrace this Law and then determine how best to use it. Let's look at a few examples that come into play every day:

1. We put a little bit of effort (either mental or physical) towards something that we want. By Law, the reaction to that little bit of effort will be a little result.

2. We put a lot of effort into eating a huge plate of fries and three burgers. By Law, the reaction is that our body will take in all the calories and convert them to energy or store them as fat.

3. We say something nasty to our partner. By Law, their reaction may be to say or do something nasty back, store it away to be expressed at a later point, become upset, or pack their bags.

What we do or say does not go away because we wish that it did. And believe me, there were plenty of times where I wished, prayed, cried, pleaded, scraped and grovelled to take back the stupid things I said or did. But the Law is impervious to emotions and the odd tantrum, and will just serve it back to us in an equal and opposite measure.

So what is a person to do? We need to wake up and become conscious of the impact that everything we do and say has on us and our life. There are consequences to the actions we take. If you do a lot of amazing and great things you will get more greatness in your life. If you are nasty and mean, even occasionally, this will come back at you. We all do dumb stuff, which has adverse consequences. So what do we do when we really screw up? We apply the *Law of Cause and Effect*. We did something negative and it had negative consequences. Now we need to do something positive, so it has a positive effect on the situation. The negative cannot be undone, but the addition of something positive can bring balance back into the situation.

I also want to talk about what happens when we complain about the results we get. A lot of us tend to blame things external to ourselves when things don't go our way, such as the government, our parents, the other driver, the stock market, the poor advice, and on and on. You are the centre of your Universe. Just as I am the centre of my Universe. When I do something, there is a cause sent out from me and I will get an equal and opposite reaction to it. In so many of the 'negative' situations in my life, when something did not work out or was a complete failure, when I consciously reviewed the situation, I saw where I made mistakes or could have made a different choice or put more effort in. Confucius said, 'In archery we have something like the way of the superior man. When the archer misses the center of the target, he turns round and seeks for the cause of his failure in himself.' To complain is to deflect personal responsibility and, even worse, to miss an opportunity to learn and grow. It is through knowledge and experience that we gain wisdom.

To round out our physics class for the day I want to briefly mention Newton's *First Law of Motion*, which is equally important when we talk about getting great results or having success in our lives. (And yes I am purposely skipping his *Second Law*, so it gives me something to write about in my next book!)

Every object in a state of uniform motion tends to remain in that state of motion unless an external force is applied to it.

It was Aristotle who first observed that objects at rest remain at rest unless a force is applied to them. Galileo expanded on the theories of inertia, which paved the way for Newton, who's First Law states that something will keep moving unless an external force is applied to it, such as friction, or wind resistance, or a concrete wall, for example. For something to begin to move takes a large amount of force to overcome inertia and create motion. So in your life, when you start doing something — practising a new skill, project, or habit — it takes a lot more effort at the start to bring the activity into motion. But the benefit here is that once something is in motion it will continue to be in motion unless acted on by an external force. And if that external force is you applying even more energy to it, the activity will gain even more momentum.

Summary

1. You can dispute or ignore universal laws of physics if you want, but they will still do what they have always done. For every action there is an equal and opposite reaction ... every time.

2. If that delicious cake you baked came out of the oven ruined and sunken

in the middle, don't blame the God of Cake Making. Objectively look at what you did or did not do that caused that result. Did you have the right ingredients? Did you follow the instructions to the letter? Did you have the right quantities? Did you perform the right actions? As I talked about in **An Introduction**, one of the essential elements to personal growth and abundance is taking personal responsibility. *A small caveat. In Chapter 21 we will talk more about that 'failure' thing. What I want you to always remember is when we make a mistake; it is something we did, or didn't do. The mistake is not who we are. Never attach yourself to the mistake. You and the mistake are two very different entities.*

3. The more effort or energy you put into something, the greater the effect and the greater the result that is possible. As a former engineer in the Australian Army, I can assure you that the more explosive we used, the bigger the bang, every time. And so it is with you — the more energy you put into a situation, the greater the result will be. But just as an engineer blowing up a bridge knows, *where you place the explosive* is just as important as having the right amount for the task. It is not just about the energy you exert, but where and how you exert it. Be very conscious about where and how you direct your energy.

4. If you make a mistake (which makes you human) then exert a positive force of good to balance out the negative that might have resulted before.

5. It takes much more effort to get something moving than it does to keep it moving. While it is harder to start something, be encouraged by the knowledge that once it's started, it's easier to keep it going. I recall reading an article that said a space ship taking off from Earth uses the same amount of fuel to overcome Earth's gravitational pull as it uses for the rest of the flight to the moon and back. Once you have overcome the main resistance in the starting process, the rest will be much easier.

6. Newton, Galileo and Aristotle were smart dudes and I thank them for their contribution to making our lives happier as we become more conscious of the thoughts we focus on, the behavior we exhibit, the choices we make

and the responses to changing circumstances we have along the way. Thanks guys!

Happiness Strategies

1. Take a break from blaming external gremlins for the next 7 days.

2. When something does not work out, look closer at what you could have done differently or better, or where your efforts might have been more usefully applied.

3. If you make a mistake, first look in the mirror and acknowledge that you are a member of Tribe Homo Sapien and that all of us in that tribe make mistakes. Then think of what 'good' action you can take to bring your life and the lives of those around you back into balance.

Brief history lesson (with no test at the end)

I wanted to end this chapter with a valuable insight that relates to all the information in this book and the level of your happiness, health, vitality and longevity.

Back in the 17th Century, around the time of Newton, a path was split in the West that is only now starting to come back together. It was decided around that time that everything that was objective and physical — the body — would be handled by science, and everything that was subjective or unseen — the mind — would be handled by the church. This created a separation between mind and body that has lasted for centuries, and still lingers today.

It is only in recent years, with new findings in quantum physics, epigenetics, biology and neuroscience by an emerging new breed of scientist, such as Dr Candace Pert, Dr Bruce Lipton, and Dr Joe Dispenza to name a few, that the separation between mind and body is closing. In fact you will start to hear the term 'mindbody' used more frequently as science comes to understand there is no gap between the mind and body. Dr Joe Dispenza, author of *Evolve Your Brain* and a key personality in the movie *What the Bleep Do We Know?*, uses the term 'causing an effect' instead of 'cause and effect' to highlight the ability that we all have to change our external world by working on our self and our internal world.

So I want you to understand, as you read through this book, that the mind greatly influences the body and the body greatly influences the mind. Your thoughts definitely affect your body and health, and your body and the emotions it is expressing definitely affect the state of your mind.

With that history lesson over and our mindbody together as one, let's get back to your daily practices for happiness.

CHAPTER 5:

Become a grand master through the power of Daily Rituals

The successful person makes a habit of doing what the failing person doesn't like to do.
Thomas Edison, American inventor and businessman

This chapter is super practical. First I talk about the magic and compounding benefit of Daily Rituals and then give you the best rituals to incorporate into your life that will make a HUGE change to your peace, vitality, stress levels and your default level of happiness. The power of specific and consistent Daily Rituals cannot be understated.

In the WorldsBIGGESTGym™ *30-Day Happiness Challenge*, one of the key strategies to achieving high success for our clients is the introduction of specific (and scientifically supported) Daily Rituals. We explain the why by using the analogy of an elite athlete. Obviously it is the result of years of concentrated and consistent effort when an elite athlete reaches the world-class level. Let's use football as an example. Compare this game of sport played at the highest level to a single day in the 'Game of Life', which we can also play at the 'elite' level. I say a single day because that is all we ever have. We can't change yesterday's score and we can't play tomorrow's game today. All we have is today.

Imagine a world cup football match between Team Life and Team Challenge. If we look more closely at one of the star players from Team Life, let's call her Prudence Beckham (no relation to David), who is a world-class and highly paid elite athlete, we notice some specific things. We notice that she performs a series of rituals before, during and after the match. Before the match she warms her body up physically and prepares herself mentally for the game, by playing it out in her mind in advance. She also makes sure she has all the necessary equipment in good working order before the game. Additionally she makes sure she is well hydrated and eats foods that will not weigh or slow her down, but will provide consistent energy during the game. She may even do some warm up drills before the day, so that her responses will come more instinctively. She will definitely start to focus on her main goal and pre-planned strategies, and block other distractions from her mind. The 'game' is all that counts.

When she actually starts playing the game she stays focused on the end goal. She constantly assesses and adjusts her tactics depending on what is needed to counter the opposition or changing circumstances. Her game is a mix of movement, pause, explosive action and retreat, but overriding it all is a focus on the end goal. She also uses the resources she has around her (the other players) to ensure they score the most goals. Throughout the game she will take rest breaks, short and longer ones, to ensure she remains as fresh as possible for the whole game. Coupled with those breaks are water breaks and maybe a high-energy snack designed to keep energy flowing for the duration of the game. If the opposition scores a goal, rather than give up, she may reassess her tactics, adjusting them as necessary, and expend a burst of energy to score a retaliatory goal.

At the end of the game, regardless of its outcome, she will look back over it to see what worked and what did not so she can improve her performance for next time; because she realizes that there are more games to come in this season and in her professional career. She will rehydrate and eat high-quality food to replace the energy that she expended and start the internal repair work on her body. And finally she will rest — for a shorter period initially and then for a longer one once everything else is taken care of.

Now let's not get caught up in *winning* or *losing* in life; it's not about that. My focus is on helping you play your best game, so that at the end of the day you have used your full potential, learned new things along the way and feel comforted to know you've played a great game to the best of your ability.

Before I give you the list of the absolute BEST Daily Rituals on the market (a.k.a. your own personal rocket fuel), here's another reason *why* they are so important. Have you heard of the 'compound effect'? I believe Mr Einstein called it one of the most powerful principles in the universe. Essentially, the compound effect means that the sum is greater than its parts — small actions build up and compound over time so that the end result is MUCH bigger than each individual part. This is how Daily Rituals work too. You may not see a big shift immediately, but over time they start stacking up on each other and compounding, so you are left with a hugely positive result for yourself. Darren Hardy, the publisher of SUCCESS magazine, wrote a book on the topic called *The Compound Effect*, which is a useful resource too.

By virtue of their being physical acts, Daily Rituals bring an immediate sense of empowerment and they are easy to bring into your life. We can consciously choose and control whether we do them. The ability to *consciously* choose makes them easier to manage than, for instance, changing the *subconscious* beliefs in our head. It is much easier for me to choose to do a 4-minute physically energizing exercise than it is to decide what monkey chatter is going to pop up in my head throughout the day. And the thing about engaging in consistent behavior is that it leads to positive habits. At a very practical level, this forms a new neural network in your mind (similar to a new software program) and creates positive feelings in your body, that eventually fire off automatically. When you behave in a new way, you inevitably get new results as well. Positive behavior = positive results.

Now that the basic reasons for conducting Daily Rituals have been covered, let's get into the BEST Daily Rituals that I practice myself and that social psychologists and researchers have found actually change people's level of happiness for the better, or create a measurable positive emotional state. The caveat I will make before we see the BEST Daily Rituals is from a quote by Jim Rohn, 'What is easy to do, is also easy not to do'. The choice is yours.

The BEST Daily Rituals (recommended by WorldsBIGGESTGym™)

1. **Conduct Morning Energization Exercises.** These exercises are loosely based on the techniques and teachings of Paramahansa Yogananda, who, as well as having a really cool name, was a key individual in introducing Yoga to the USA, and author of the classic book, *Autobiography of a Yogi*. The exercises take 3 to 4 minutes and beat the heck out of coffee for waking you up in the morning: they energize body and mind, increase blood flow and kick-start metabolism. I recommend postponing your cup of coffee till afterwards; you may not feel as desperate a need for it. For a video of this gem of a workout, go to *www.theguidebooktohappiness.com*. This simple little routine is a life-changer.

2. **Practice Gratitude**. This incredibly simple 1-minute exercise will have profound affects on your psychological and emotional state. It is merely a matter of stating all of the things you are grateful for in life. Say 'thank you' — for the roof over your head, the clothes on your back, the food in the fridge, the air you breathe, the eyes you see with, the beauty of a sunrise, the gentle breeze that is cooling you, the money that allows you to buy things, your friends and family — anything and everything you can think of. I recommend doing this first thing in the morning, and saying it aloud or writing it down. This is an excellent activity for children to learn from an early age and will greatly contribute to building up their optimism muscles.

3. **Meditate**. Where do I start? This is THE BEST thing you can do for your mind and body. Numerous studies have been done on the benefits of meditation in its various forms. Dr Herbert Bensen, an Associate Professor

of Medicine at Harvard Medical School, is one of hundreds of people that have been researching and reporting on the positive effects of meditation (he calls it the *Relaxation Response*). Physically recorded benefits include reducing blood pressure, slowing the heart rate, getting deeper sleep and reducing muscle tension, to mention just a few. The emotional benefits include an increase in focus and concentration, better tolerance to stress and enhanced feelings of connectedness and harmony. Meditation has been described as a cleansing shower for the mind. Dr Bensen also suggests that meditation for 12 to 15 minutes each day is highly effective. So you do not need to sit in the lotus posture for hours to get the amazing benefits from meditation. See **Recommended reference material** for a list of helpful books about meditation. Meditation can and will change your life.

4. **Visualize and feel the attainment of your Primary Goal**. Specifically visualize your Primary Goal every day and feel the emotions you will experience when you achieve it. Without a clear goal you cannot work out your priorities for the day, which is essential to living a life of design versus living a life of chance. Remember our elite athlete? How would she play if she did not know what her goal was? She would be running all over the field with no focus or direction and at the end of the game she would not know how she fared.

5. **Listen to, or read, inspiring material**. I recommend spending at least 15 minutes each day on this ritual. Imagine if during a rest break in the game, our elite athlete, instead of listening to what her highly experienced coach had to say, sat and read a gossip magazine or listened to what the crowd was shouting out. Do you think she's going to the best sources of information on how to improve her game, or employ the best strategies, or try a new tactic? Most certainly not. To get ahead in your game of life, be SELECTIVE — seek out the best books, coaches, and audio or video training programs — immerse yourself in the good stuff. Watching the daily news is hardly likely to expand your consciousness or take you to your next level of potential.

6. **Alkalize and energize your body with a daily Green Drink (or Green Smoothie).** For this ritual, first we need to think back to those boring (well for me anyway) chemistry lessons where we learnt about the pH levels of different liquids. Acids have a pH from 1.0 to 6.9 with a pH of 1.0 being the most acidic. Water is neutral at a pH of 7.0 and everything above 7.0 is alkaline. Our body's ideal pH balance is slightly alkaline at about 7.4 pH. That is, our body's health is maintained when it is in a slightly alkaline state. The food and fluids we put into our bodies have a significant impact on controlling the pH balance. You want to consume a lot more alkaline-forming foods (fresh vegetables and fruit) than acid-forming foods (dairy, meat products, caffeine, alcohol, etc.). One way to get an awesome load of alkaline foods into your body is to have a morning Green Drink. And not surprisingly, most of these high-alkaline food sources are extremely high in nutrients that repair and maintain the body's internal health. Forgive my standing on a soapbox and delivering this next comment through a loudspeaker. Drinking a daily Green Drink has a phenomenal return on investment!! If you take nothing else from this book, take this: Adding a daily Green Drink to your life will change your health, vitality, longevity and beauty, plus take your energy to whole new level. For details on how to make a Green Drink check out *www.theguidebooktohappiness.com.*

There are a number of other highly effective Daily Rituals, but the ones above are the best you can employ right now. In the WorldsBIGGESTGym™ *30-Day Happiness Challenge*, Daily Rituals play a huge part in increasing clients' overall levels of success. When you introduce highly positive Daily Rituals and choose your daily habits, you effectively create a new way of being. You become someone more and therefore you can achieve goals at a higher level than you ever thought possible. This is one of the ways that you become the person you need to become to achieve the things you want to achieve. Change is inevitable and necessary to get more results and happiness in your life.

Summary

1. A day in your 'game of life' is like our elite athlete's match day. She practices rituals before, during and after the game to ensure she performs consistently at a high level. To have a high-performance day, you can also introduce positive and powerful rituals into your life.

2. Mastery is achieved by consistent (and persistent) actions practiced daily.

3. The *compound effect* means that the overall effect on your life of consistently practicing Daily Rituals is far greater than the total effort required to practice them.

4. We can consciously choose and perform Daily Rituals far easier than we can our thoughts. And by physically and consistently performing our Daily Rituals, we establish lifelong positive habits that are imbedded deep in our subconscious mind and help us achieve our goals.

5. Just like our elite athlete conducts a series of rituals to help her maintain that million-dollar contract, if you want to be an elite performer in life, practicing Daily Rituals makes a real difference to your results and improves your health and well-being.

6. You now have 6 easy Daily Rituals that I strongly advise you to incorporate into your daily life. You have everything to gain!

Happiness Strategies

1. For the next 7 days choose one Daily Ritual and do it every day.

2. Then for the following 7 days add a second Daily Ritual to your first and do both of them every day.

3. Then for the next 4 weeks, add an additional Daily Ritual each week, until at the end of 6 weeks, you are doing all 6 of the Daily Rituals.

Note:

You can have a rest day from your rituals one day a week if you like. But you might find you don't want to!

CHAPTER 6:

Is that really what you want to know?

There are no right answers to wrong questions.
Ursula K Le Guin, American author and poet

What object is described below?

1. I provide an answer for the questions that I am asked.
2. I don't decide right from wrong; I just answer the question.
3. I am really good at coming up with answers because I have vast amounts of information and stored data to draw upon.
4. If the question is wrong, I will give the wrong answer (or no answer at all).

You guessed it — it's a computer. A computer can perform all the functions described above. But what else has the same functions? The human mind; the brain in action. When your mind answers the questions it is asked, it generally does not judge the quality of the question, but draws on vast amounts of information but unlike our computer it will keep processing a question until it finds an answer.

If the human mind is like a computer (though much more powerful), then the most important thing you can do to get the right answer is to ask the right question. If I wanted to find out how to get rid of fleas on dogs, what are the chances of my finding the answer if I search using the phrase *common breeds of dogs in Tibet*? Pretty much zero.

Let's stick with the computer analogy. Have you ever searched the internet for two completely opposite points of view on a topic? The computer does not tell you which view is morally, factually, or intuitively 'right', it just gives you the information it has access to. A search on the topic of eating olive oil yields a large number of articles extolling its health benefits; but it also yields articles arguing that it's not good for you due to its high fat content and lack of fibre and should thus be consumed sparingly. What you look for is what you will find, so it pays to ask a question as specifically and as beneficially as possible — if you look for the positive, or the negative, in any given situation you will find it.

Let me show you how this applies to you and your happiness. Read the two questions below. Which choice of words makes you feel better about yourself, puts you in a peak emotional state and positively affects your behavior?

1. Why am I so overweight and unfit?

2. How can I lose weight and increase my fitness?

That amazing mind of yours that is far more effective than the average super computer is going to start giving you lots of answers to the above questions — but the answers will be very different depending on which question you asked.

While the first question focuses on the PROBLEM, the second one focuses on the SOLUTION. Earl Nightingale, in his *Lead the Field* personal development program suggested, 'The difference between a successful person and an unsuccessful person is not that the successful person has no problems; it is that the successful person focuses on finding solutions to their problems'. How? By asking better questions.

Because your mind will answer the questions you ask it without judgment, it is far more beneficial to ask solution-oriented questions. By improving the quality of the question we ask, we will effectively improve the answer and therefore the results we get.

Taking the above example deeper, of the two questions below, which would that brilliant mind of yours answer more usefully for your life?

1. How can I lose weight and increase my fitness?

2. How can I lose 10 kg (22 pounds) and improve the time it takes me to run 5 km (3 miles) by the end of the year?

It is worth taking the time to ask the right question so when your brain kicks into gear it is heading in the right direction. Telling the taxi driver to drive north might get you close, but telling him or her the exact address will guarantee you reach your desired destination.

Tony Robbins, one of the best success coaches on the planet, suggests taking this solution-oriented technique even one step further by adding to the end of your question '… and have fun at the same time?' Again your amazing brain will click into gear and start providing you with ways to lose your weight, improve your fitness and do it in a fun way. Ask a better question and you get a better answer.

Remember when we were growing up, we were told 'you can have the blue one OR the red one, but not both'? Well now that you are grown up, you don't have to do the 'and/or' thing if you don't want to. You can ask a much better question, such as: 'How can I get a higher paying job and have more time off, while enjoying all aspects of my life?' The potential answer is inside you and the better you get at asking specific, solution-oriented questions, the better your life will become.

Summary

To get the best possible results in your life it is imperative that you ask the best possible questions you can, to tap into the power of your amazing mind. And remember:

1. If you don't like the answers you are getting, then change the questions.

2. Always ask SOLUTION-oriented questions.

3. Add to the end of your question 'and how can I have fun while doing this?' You will be surprised at what you can dream up when given the chance to tap into your inherent creativity.

4. You don't have to choose A *or* B. Maybe there is a way for you to have both A *and* B. Just ask the question and see what solutions you come up with.

Happiness Strategies

1. Determine one of your goals.

2. At the top of the page in your journal or whiteboard, write your solution-oriented question, 'How can I achieve [insert your goal] and have fun at the same time?'

3. Write down 10 to 15 things you can do that will help you achieve your goal to the standard and within the timeframe you want while having fun at the same time.

4. Do Steps 1 to 3 for 10 to 15 minutes, every day, from Monday to Friday and you will not only achieve that goal, but you will increase your thinking power for all other thought processes you engage in.

CHAPTER 7:

I could complain, or I could just enjoy myself

He who cannot dance claims the floor is uneven.
Proverb

'Now here's the thing,' as Randy Jackson often says on *American Idol*; by consciously avoiding the act of complaining, you will not only make a *little* difference to your life, you might also manage to change your whole life. It has a lot to do with how the mind works. And since you are now becoming a bit of an expert on that topic after reading Chapter 1 on the relationship between the conscious and subconscious mind, we can jump straight into how, by not complaining, you can change your life.

You know I like to ask you questions — it gets that magnificent brain of yours working — so here is the million-dollar question in this life-changing chapter: What are you focusing on when you complain?
Is the answer:

a.   The thing that you ***don't*** want to happen? or

b.   The thing that you ***do*** want to happen?

You guessed it! Complaining only increases your focus on what you don't want in your life. Does this scenario sound familiar? 'The staff at the supermarket were so rude to me today. Then when I was driving home, everyone kept getting in my way and this car almost ran into me. And then I ran out of gas! I had to call someone to bring me more just so I could get home. And then when I got home, there were a mountain of chores to do. And then ...'

All the energy being poured into this story is convincing your *non-judgmental* subconscious mind that the more drama you have in your life, the better. It works to deliver more to you, drawing you towards similar situations and other people who like to create dramas. Let me assure you: There are much better ways than this to be noticed and feel the love and connection that you are ultimately searching for.

I have worked with a number of clients that have associated drama with love. They feel that if they create a big enough drama (note the word 'create') then people will notice them. We can easily create drama from everyday situations. Take the following examples:

- 'I got absolutely no sleep last night!' Reality: you got about 4 hours sleep. This is not ideal but you're unlikely to die of sleep deprivation any time soon.

- 'Every car on the road was trying to ram into me on the way home.' Reality: 3 cars out of the 973 that you passed on the way home were closer than you were comfortable with.

- 'This is the worst restaurant service that I have ever experienced in my life.' Reality: The order you made was slow to come out and they gave you French fries instead of potato wedges. Plus the waiter mixed up your drinks with the table beside it (before fixing the order).

It is amazing what we can let bother us when we feed negative energy into something that does not go exactly our way. I love the work of Byron Katie, author of *Loving What Is*. She says, 'When I argue with reality, I lose. But only 100% of the time.' So when the waiter brings you a cappuccino that is too cold, complaining about the reality of the situation will not make it any different. The thing that will invariably fix this life-threatening situation (oops, there goes my Australian sarcasm again) is to say, 'Excuse me. My cappuccino is too cold, could you warm it up for me please?' Problem solved and ulcer averted.

I am joking around a little bit here, but let me be clear about the real downsides of complaining:

1. Your good-quality friends will avoid you because you are not much fun to be around.

2. Other people that enjoy complaining will be attracted to you, making your leisure time rather miserable and taking you in the opposite direction to self-improvement and growth.

3. The act of complaining is likely to make you angry or upset or frustrated, which if practiced on a regular basis will affect your health. Harboring negative emotions can cause more acid to be created in your body (which can lead to ulcers, digestion problems, etc.). Your stomach is likely to become contracted therefore adversely affecting the depth of your breathing (meaning less O_2 is getting to your hungry little cells). Plus you are likely to create excess tension in your muscles, which might cause muscular aches and pains and poor circulation.

4. Your super-powerful subconscious mind will think you want things to go wrong so will help you lose focus and concentration and be easily distracted, and will send out a signal to the world that you would like to regularly have something to complain about. Remember that the subconscious mind does not judge — it just delivers.

Writing about the physical side effects of complaining or harboring negative emotions reminds me of a situation I see quite often. A lot of people that I have worked with over the years have had stomach or digestion issues. After I talk to them about better nutritional choices I ask them to describe at a very basic level the role of the stomach and digestive system. I then give them my version. The role of the stomach and digestive system is to take what it is given, absorb as many nutrients as it can, and then let the waste pass through to the bowels. Accept the good and let the bad pass you by. Sounds like a pretty good way to live life, don't you think?

Think back to the scenario from the start of the chapter. How would you tell it if you had to focus only on the positive elements? What could you have done differently to have brought more calmness to yourself and others? The staff member at the supermarket was rude, but that couldn't have been about you — you behaved politely and didn't give them added stress, so let it go. On the drive home, you were feeling stressed and anxious about being late to your next errand. No one was getting in your way — everyone was also going about their busy days and doing their best to deal with the traffic. Perhaps next time you could enjoy the peace of being inside the car and breathe deeply till your next appointment or listen to some great personal growth material while you drive. You ran out of gas — wasn't it lucky that you had your phone on you to call for help? And that no one ran into you while your car was stalled? In every situation, there is something positive to take from it if you choose to focus on it.

Will Bowen is a pastor in the USA. His book, *A Complaint Free World*, outlines an interesting challenge: go for 21 consecutive days without complaining, criticizing or gossiping. It is MUCH harder than you'd think. Or maybe you are thinking the opposite, 'how the heck could I do that?!' With most people, Bowen found it took between 4 and 6 months to be able to go 21 consecutive days without complaining, criticizing or gossiping. He also found, and was validated by the millions of people that have taken up the challenge, that when you stop complaining, criticizing and gossiping (and stick to reality), the dramas in your life seem to disappear, your negative emotions take a back seat and more harmony seems to flow into your life.

By being truthful about a given situation, rather than exaggerating it and complaining, you will also find that the emotional intensity of that situation will be greatly reduced, allowing you to come up with a more logical and often more creative solution to the challenge that you might be facing.

Summary

1. Complaining is focusing your mind's power on the things that you don't want (more of) in your life. The more energy you direct at something the bigger it grows.

2. Complaining causes negative emotions, which can be detrimental to your health.

3. People who accept what is and avoid complaining are much more fun to be around.

4. As Byron Katie tells us, if you argue with reality you will lose 100% of the time.

5. Complaining does not fix things. Funnily enough, fixing things fixes things!

Happiness Strategies

1. Instead of complaining, exaggerating for negative effect, criticizing or gossiping over the next week, stick to the plain old facts that are 100% true, 100% of the time.

2. Go to *www.acomplaintfreeworld.org* and take the 21-Day Challenge (which takes much longer than 21 days to complete).

3. Know at the deepest level that rather than enriching or improving your life, complaining is only making it less fun. Choose a new habit. Focus on what is positive in each situation.

CHAPTER 8:

Gratitude is the wonder drug of the 21st century

Let us rise up and be thankful, for if we didn't learn a lot today, at least we learned a little, and if we didn't learn a little, at least we didn't get sick, and if we got sick, at least we didn't die; so, let us all be thankful.
Buddha, spiritual leader on whose teachings Buddhism was founded

Gratitude is the wonder drug of the 21st century because it has absolutely no negative side effects. None. Nada. Zip. Zilch. It also has one of the biggest returns on investment of any happiness strategy you decide to incorporate into your life. Practicing gratitude is ridiculously good for your body, mind and soul. And just in case you're not yet convinced (and before I get into the scientific research supporting this great practise), let me introduce three volunteers who are going to highlight for you the power of gratitude in a typical daily setting. Please make welcome Maximus (forgive me, I just watched *Gladiator*), Daisy and Jimmy.

Here is the scenario. I receive some unexpected money from a lotto I entered, and decide to share my good fortune by presenting each of my friends, Maximus, Jimmy and Daisy, with a freshly minted $20 note. Maximus says, 'Thanks' with a big smile on his face. Jimmy says, 'Only $20?' while sporting a disdainful look on his face. And finally, Daisy says, 'Thanks so much. This is awesome. You are the best. Thank you so much' and not only genuinely smiles but engages me in a rigorous two-handed handshake for a good 10 seconds —

which is a long time for a rigorous handshake.

Now here comes the million-dollar question: If I only have one $20 note next time, who am I *most likely* to give it to? Maximus, Jimmy or Daisy?

I am sure you too would give the money to the person that is most GRATEFUL. In this case it is the hand-pumping Daisy. In fact you would probably even go out of your way to give the $20 to Daisy. People who are most grateful are likely to have others go to some effort to give them things because they allow the person doing the giving to experience a physical as well as an emotional high; the brain will actually cause the production and release of 'feel-good' chemicals.

To take this principle further, I suggest that life, source, the universe, God, or whichever word you prefer to use, might be working on a very similar principle. The most grateful people in life tend to attract more and more goodness, while the most ungrateful and miserable people tend to attract very little to no goodness. Also, whom do you most enjoy hanging out, helping, being friends, or doing business with? The person who is grateful for your help, friendship, or business, or that ungrateful and consistently complaining person in the corner?

Robert A Emmons is a University of California Professor of Psychology and author of the best-selling book, *Thanks! How the New Science of Gratitude Can Make You Happier*. Emmons found that people who view life as a gift and consciously acquire an 'attitude of gratitude' would experience multiple advantages.

In an experimental comparison (conducted by Emmons and his associate, Michael E McCullough, in 2003), those who kept gratitude journals on a weekly basis were found to exercise more regularly, reported fewer physical symptoms, felt better about their lives as a whole, and felt more optimistic about the upcoming week compared to those who recorded hassles or neutral life events. A related benefit was observed in the realm of personal goal attainment: Participants who kept gratitude lists were more likely to have made progress towards important personal goals (academic, interpersonal and health-based) over a 2-month period compared to people in the other experimental conditions.

Other reasons to feel grateful

Have you ever tried to feel grateful and depressed at the same time? I want you to think of all the things you are grateful for in your life — the roof (or the sky) over your head, the money you used to buy food this week, the good people in your life, the free air that you are breathing, your heart that is beating, the friend you called this morning, and the list goes on. While you focus on all of these great things I want you to feel depressed. Now don't stop imagining the great stuff. Keep the great stuff in mind and try as hard as you can to feel like crap. It is pretty much impossible to do. Essentially, a positive and a negative emotion cannot co-exist at the same time in your mind. You can choose to be grateful OR miserable — but you cannot be both at the same time!

Practicing gratitude is one of THE EASIEST practises you can do and has the greatest possible positive impact on your life (as suggested in Chapter 4 on Daily Rituals). All you need to do is ask that brilliant computer-like mind of yours, 'What am I or can I be grateful for in my life right now?' and then let it start spitting out answers. The great thing is, the more you practise, the better you become at easily identifying the blessings in your life. Your gratitude muscle is definitely one that you want to work out on a daily basis for best effect.

Imagine what it would be like if you trained your brain (or the brain of your daughter or son) to automatically identify the *good* in life, or in a particular situation. What do you think you are most likely to find? You guessed it — all the good stuff. As a result, you are also likely to feel better, and may even find yourself smiling more often, feeling a positive vibrational field around yourself, and you may suddenly be a whole lot more attractive to potential partners, in love and business, and to your family and friends. In fact, this gratitude thing may even make you more money. Sounds good to me.

I personally believe one of the big differences between an optimist and a pessimist is the predominant question they have playing in their mind. Out of the two options below I am sure that you can figure out which question is asked by the optimist and which is by the pessimist:

1. What is wrong or could go wrong in this situation?

2. What is great or could be great in this situation?

As you can imagine, the answers and more importantly the resultant feelings associated with those answers are going to be significantly different for each question. I am not suggesting that you bury your head in the sand, but when you consciously look for the good in a situation, even in a situation that appears awful at first glance, you will find the gold at the bottom of the pan and recognize lessons to learn to benefit your life.

Practicing and expressing gratitude puts you into a positive emotional state, which tends to relax your body, allowing more breath to be drawn in, the blood to flow easier, and the heart to beat slower. Our body can do that self-healing thing it does so well when it's in a state of emotional stability. Also, in this relaxed state, you are likely to be more creative and solution-oriented. Let's face it. We all have problems in our lives, so the better we become at finding high-quality solutions, the better our lives will become.

Summary

1. The person who is the most grateful gets more.

2. Don't hold back on saying 'thank you'.

3. It is pretty much impossible to be extremely grateful and depressed at the same time.

4. Practicing gratitude is like using a muscle: the more you practice it, the better and stronger you become, and the easier it is to do. Remember to make practicing gratitude a Daily Ritual.

5. Practicing gratitude conditions your mind to look for the good or positive benefits in any situation.

6. Being grateful is most likely to put you into a positive emotional state, which will positively impact on your emotional and physical health (as studies by Professor Emmons, among others, indicate).

Happiness Strategies

Practicing gratitude takes less than 2 minutes a day to perform and provides you with a remarkably disproportionate amount of positive benefit for your investment.

1. Make the practice of gratitude a Daily Ritual (best done first thing in the morning and last thing at night), by either saying (preferably aloud) to yourself or writing down in a journal 5 to 10 things, or as many things as you can think of in 2 minutes, that you are grateful for.

2. Become an expert at saying, 'Thank you very much', 'I really appreciate what you have done for me', 'Thank you, life (or God, the Universe, Mother Nature, Infinite Intelligence, etc.).'

CHAPTER 9:

The science of breath

Breath is the bridge which connects life to consciousness,
which unites your body to your thoughts.
Thich Nhat Hanh

I think we can agree that none of us is going to experience a life filled with happiness without having the breathing thing going on. Of all the ways we can maintain, let alone extend and optimize, our life breathing holds the number one spot. No food for *weeks* and we die. No water for *days* and we die. No oxygen for just a few *minutes* and we die. If we want to live, we must breathe. Therefore, consciously optimizing the way we breathe is essential to increasing our level of happiness (and health).

For us to be truly happy, alive, vibrant and energized, it is imperative that we understand and increase the functioning of our breathing so that we bring the absolute most oxygen into the lungs and cells of our bodies.

Too often we give limited or no thought to breathing because we have been taught that it is an involuntary action of the body, therefore we don't need to worry about it. But the Indian yogis, who spent their lives practicing the art and science of various forms of yoga, knew there was more to it than that and devoted centuries of study and practice to the art and science of breathing, giving them a lot of street cred on the topic. And as a result of their matrimony with the breath, these yogis were able to achieve astounding physical feats, including:

- Overcoming pain and contorting their bodies into pretzels.

- Going for unexpectedly long periods of time without drawing a breath.

- Slowing down the heart rate until the heart stopped beating (yet still remaining conscious).

- Being unaffected by experiencing extreme cold (or other forms of pain) for extended periods of time.

- Meditating to such a deep level that a gun shot fired beside the ear yielded no physical reaction (including micro facial movements that were considered involuntary).

Understanding what happens when you breathe may help. Consciously improving the functioning of your breathing will result in more oxygen traveling to the brain, lungs, heart and brain cells allowing them to generate even more energy, thus increasing focus, concentration, memory and even self-control. The body engages three parts to draw in breath:

1. The diaphragm — when we breathe in (preferably through the nose to allow the nasal hairs and lining in the nasal passage to trap any dust, and to warm and moisten the air before it enters the lungs), the stomach is expanded and the diaphragm activated, creating a vacuum that draws air into the lower part of the lungs.

2. The ribs — the floating ribs activate to expand the chest cavity, creating a vacuum that draws air into the middle part of the lungs.

3. The shoulders — when we shrug our shoulders, we create another vacuum in our chest cavity and draw air into the upper part of our lungs.

When the lungs are full (and the air is within the many alveoli, which are small, grape-like sacs in the lungs) the blood vessels that weave their way through the lungs pick up the oxygen molecules through infusion, attach them to blood platelets and then allow the oxygen to be transported through the body to all of our cells.

The diaphragm, the ribs and the shoulder shrug are listed in order of their effectiveness and importance. The diaphragm has no other function to perform apart from creating a vacuum to fill the lungs with air. Since it is purpose-built for this task, the diaphragm is the first thing we need to engage when breathing, then the ribs, and lastly the shoulder shrug.

However, I have found that when asked to take a deep breath, the first thing most people do is lift their shoulders, then expand their ribs, and disregard the diaphragm. In my mind that is like taking the B and C Grade teams to the World Championships. You might do all right, but you are much more likely to win if you take along your A team, which in this case is Team Diaphragm. It might not look pretty, but it is expert at what it does!

The problem for a lot of us is our habit of sucking in our stomach (so we don't look fat) and puffing our chest out. This means that we're hampering the function of the diaphragm. To get the most air and O_2 into our bodies we need to regain control of the stomach and let the diaphragm do what it does best. If you breathe an extra 10 to 20% of air into your lungs, you are effectively providing an extra 10 to 20% of oxygen for every cell in your body.

The brain uses over 20% of the oxygen that comes into the body to maintain its functions. Our muscle cells also need oxygen to burn fat or glycogen (carbohydrates) and produce energy to make our muscles function more effectively — and the more prolonged our physical activity is, the more oxygen we require. To burn fat requires more oxygen, so if the oxygen getting into your body is limited, it might actually affect your ability to burn off fat and thus your overall weight management. Convinced yet?

If we want to achieve the greatest results in life, we need the greatest amount of energy we can access. Our brain and muscles must have the greatest amount of oxygen that we can give them. Put simply:

MORE OXYGEN = MORE effective production of ENERGY

Now that we understand a little better how the respiratory system functions, how do we breathe to get more air into our lungs and have more energy? The yogis (who I like to call the pioneers in the practise and research of breath) call a big breath a *full yogic breath* and it goes something like this:

1. Stand or sit up straight (but not rigidly).

2. Expand your stomach at the same time as you focus your attention on the air entering your nose. Draw in the air until you feel that the stomach is fully and naturally expanded. (You don't need to push out your stomach as if you are entering a big-belly contest.)

3. Next, feel your chest cavity expanding as you use the intercostal muscles between your ribs and imagine your lungs expanding too.

4. Finally, subtly shrug your shoulders to get air into the last part of the lungs (the upper extremity).

5. Follow the same order (lower, middle and upper) as you breathe out, and then repeat.

Just doing this breathing exercise for a few minutes a few times a day will energize and vitalize your body and mind.

Another benefit of breathing properly is that it softens and massages the stomach and internal organs. This is very important if you experience stress. Using the diaphragm to breathe relaxes the stomach, which aids digestion and reduces the likelihood of indigestion or poor digestion. Have you noticed that when you are feeling stressed you tend to breathe more shallowly; that is, take smaller, shorter breaths? This is because the stomach is often contracted and tense, restricting your ability to use it fully to breathe. Doing breathing exercises is one of the strategies to overcoming and managing stress because it relaxes the stomach, deepens the breath and energizes the body. Next time you feel stressed I recommend that you get comfortable, focus on relaxing the stomach and then do 5 to 10 full yogic breaths. You will be amazed at what a difference it makes!

Hello to a lot more happiness, health, longevity, peace, tranquillity and mental clarity, to name just a few of the remarkable benefits of breathing fully and properly.

Summary

1. Breathing is the most important thing we do, so it is in our best interest to master it. Our life, not to mention our happiness and health, depends on it.

2. We use three parts of our bodies to breathe: the diaphragm, the floating ribs and the shoulders. Use all three, in that order.

3. Sending out Team Diaphragm first is the best choice if you want to succeed at the highest level.

4. MORE OXYGEN = MORE ENERGY = BIGGER & BETTER RESULTS.

5. Using the stomach to breathe also softens and massages the internal organs, which aids the digestion process (another important life, and therefore happiness, function).

6. Relax the stomach if you feel stressed, which allows deeper breathing and improves the digestive process.

Happiness Strategies

1. Practice the *full yogic breath*. Breathing in through your nose, allow your lower lungs to fill by the use of your diaphragm (letting your stomach slightly protrude as you do so), then use your floating ribs to draw air into the middle lungs and finally the upper chest to fill the last part of the lungs. Do this exercise while sitting up straight, standing (with hands resting on the navel) or lying down. Do this in the morning and at night (5 to 20 controlled breaths) or at times when you feel stressed. Stay aware of your breath and body.

2. Join a yoga or meditation class a couple of times a week. But be warned. It will definitely improve the quality of your life.

CHAPTER 10:

One of the greatest virtues on Earth

When in doubt, tell the truth.
Mark Twain, American author and humorist

Have you ever wished you could have the super-human strength of Superman? As a young child of 43 years of age, I am a big fan and believe that of all the super heroes, Superman most resoundingly epitomizes the higher virtues of humanity. He is honest (aside from wearing the glasses and persona of a complete klutz), kind, compassionate, modest, humble, focused on the greater good, courageous, persistent, loving, open, caring and an all-round good guy. So how would you like to become a superman or superwoman in your own life? To have incredible powers and strengths in the face of adversity? Are you ready to step up and receive super powers that will not require you to be bitten by a spider, infused with gamma radiation, or born on a distant planet?

If it is not right do not do it; if it is not true do not say it.
Marcus Aurelius, Roman Emperor

Have you ever heard of an Olympic Gold Medallist that reached the world stage by putting in absolutely no effort? If it took no effort it would be rather crowded on that winners' podium. To be a winner in life you actually have to expend some energy and effort to get to where you want to be. Although I might be able to give you the knowledge of how to be a superwoman or superman, it will require effort on your part to fully realize.

The virtue I am talking about, that underlies so many other virtues, is the virtue of *integrity*. If you have never thought about it specifically or placed a lot of value in it, then you might just be missing one of the major ingredients to a more fulfilling life, greater success and a whole lot more happiness, in addition to much less stress and pain.

Before I delve deeper into the theory on how to become a superperson, I would like you to perform a little physical activity. You will need a partner to get the most out of this, so grab the closest person and tell them that you will need their assistance for the next 2 minutes. If you are riding public transport as you read this be sure to ask nicely. If you live on an island and there is not a single person around you for miles, bookmark this page and come back to the exercise later. But please do it! I want more happy people on the planet.

Kinaesthetic exercise

1. Ask your newfound (or existing) friend to hold out their arm in front of themselves horizontally (parallel to the ground or floor of the plane, train or bus) with the hand open and the palm facing down. If there isn't much room, they can bend their arm at the elbow, but their forearm must be parallel to the ground.

2. Instruct them to hold their arm as strongly as possible so it is rigid.

3. Place your hand on top of theirs (lucky you) and push down on it. The aim is to feel how much force they are exerting or how strong they are in resisting your downward force.

4. Ask them to say their name aloud. For example, if I was your partner I would say, 'My name is Carl Massy'. Then push down on their hand again and feel the force they generate.

5. Lastly, ask them to give you a false name, such as 'My name is Mickey

Mouse'. Then push down on their hand again and feel the force they generate.

You will find that when they say their real name (unless that dodgy stranger was making up a fake name to begin with) their arm strength and power will be strong. And amazingly enough, when they say the fake name they will have a lot less strength and power to hold their arm rigid. It seems that when you are telling the truth you have more (measurable) physical strength; being honest makes you more powerful; living a life of high integrity makes you a force to be reckoned with — not too dissimilar from a superperson.

Tip: Doing this exercise is a great way to tell if your son or daughter really did take a cookie out of the cookie jar. You now have your very own 'lie detector' strategy.

Doing this simple exercise reminds you that you have more strength and power when you are honest and come from a place of integrity. And that is why for thousands of years, the greatest philosophers and thought-leaders have talked about the virtue of integrity. If we are not living a life based on integrity, then we may only be working at 70% of our potential strength. Imagine if you were 30% stronger in your life — what more could you achieve? It is definitely worth tapping into that power source.

You know how we talked about how you would have to do some work? Well now I am going to tell you how you can do less work and become happier. Read the scenario below. How much effort do you think it would take to reach the correct answer?

Scenario: Look at 15 coloring pencils arranged in order on a table for 30 seconds. Then watch the television for 15 minutes. Walk outside for 5 minutes. Recite the alphabet twice. Then come back to the table where the pencils have been all been mixed up and recall the order in which they were originally placed.

Telling untruths or lies is like trying to remember what order we left the pencils in — it takes time and measurable mental energy to do so. Whereas telling the truth is just seeing things for what they are — it requires far less energy and time. You don't have to second guess the truth; it is right there in front of you. Not telling the truth uses up your current quota of energy that would be better used to achieve the things you want in your life. The easy path, in the end, is telling the truth. Though at the time it might seem harder, telling the truth is going to save you tonnes of energy with which to play the real game of life.

When I talk about honesty and integrity I am not just talking about when you deal with other people. One of the most important people in your life, I would suggest the most important, is yourself. If you lie to yourself, then you are reducing your strength and power. If you tell yourself that when your friend said something nasty to you 'it did not hurt' when it actually did, you are lying to yourself. The truth is it did hurt and therefore you probably need to tell them so (or *unfriend* them on Facebook at the very least!). Telling yourself that it does not matter if you don't get an A grade on your exam, when it really does matter, is not going to make you stronger, but weaker. You cannot lie to yourself and think that there is no price to pay. The formula will still be this: lie = less power (whether you believe it or not). Plus, you cannot get away from yourself. You can't tell yourself a lie and then change countries and expect the lie not to follow you. It would be nice if it worked that way, but let me assure you as a frequent traveler, any lie I tell myself follows me everywhere I go.

You also cannot be completely honest in 90% of your life's dealings and dishonest in 10% and expect that the 10% will not affect the whole. One rotten apple spoils the whole bunch. To use a more extreme example (sorry in advance), it would be like having a badly infected sore on your left arm and believing that it won't affect the rest of your body if you do nothing about it. Left untreated, eventually the toxins in the sore will make their way into the bloodstream and poison the rest of the body. I don't mean to be a drama queen here, but I do mean to highlight that we need to practice integrity in ALL areas of our life if we want to have access to 100% of the energy that we have at our disposal.

In looking for people to hire, you look for three qualities: integrity, intelligence, and energy. And if they don't have the first, the other two will kill you.
Warren Buffet, American business magnate and philanthropist

Summary

1. If you want to be a superperson then remember you have a lot more strength when you are telling the truth.

2. It takes more energy, concentration and effort to tell lies. If your goal is to find the person or job of your dreams, then take the easy option and start telling the truth.

3. Lying to yourself is not good business since you hang out with you 24/7. And escaping to an island is not going to save you from yourself or any lies that you tell.

4. You cannot be dishonest in one part of your life and not have it affect the other parts. The best policy is to maintain high integrity in all areas of your life.

Happiness Strategies

1. If you did not do the **kinaesthetic exercise** part way through the chapter, stop and do it now, or in the next 24 hours. And if you meet the person of your dreams in asking a complete stranger to help you do this exercise, I would like an invite to the engagement party (and can I bring one guest along as well?)

2. For the rest of this month I want you to overcompensate by being 100% honest with every person that you deal with. Here comes another caveat: I

am not responsible for any slaps, kicks, punches, sneers, flying frying pans or other projectiles launched at you, or for any physical harm that may occur, as a result of your being 100% honest for the said period.

3. If you need some motivation on being 100% honest, I recommend that you watch the Ricky Gervais movie, *The Invention of Lying*.

4. Do not assume that someone does not need to hear or cannot handle hearing the truth from us. Who are we to know what is required for the bigger picture in their life and for them to be the best person they can be? So when someone asks, 'Do you like this music I have created after slaving away on it for the last 6 months?' it might be in their best interest for you to tell them, 'Actually, if I was to be 100% honest with you, and this is only my unqualified opinion, I personally don't like the music. But that is just my opinion.' This might lead the person to consider their target market more closely and ensure that the marketing effort is better directed to it. In the end, your being honest may end up making them an extra $100,000 in sales!

CHAPTER 11:

Values-based decision making

Our problem is not to find better values but to be faithful to those we profess.

John W Gardner, American educator

While this chapter focuses on values, I want to briefly touch on spirituality, a place from where many of our values come. I believe spirituality is absolutely essential for a heightened level of sustained happiness, particularly through the setbacks we all inevitably face in life. If you believe that life is for you and not against you and that life (or God, Allah, the Universe, Mother Earth, etc.) loves you unconditionally then you are given a great sense of personal power in any moment, not just on your birthday or on Valentine's Day, or when some other external source provides you with positive reinforcement. Having a strong spiritual life reminds you that you are worthy of being loved and being happy every day. It is interesting to note that the more Einstein understood the universe and its laws, the deeper his spiritual beliefs became.

Even though I do not delve too deeply into spirituality here, I am calling this the *spiritual* chapter (so I can say that we worked on the body, mind and spirit throughout this book!). I have only dedicated one chapter to it, because the topic can and does fill numerous books by itself. In **Recommended reference material** I have listed some of the great teachers I have followed and great books I have read, and I encourage you to read these. Also do your own research and inner exploration to find answers to the spiritual questions you may have.

Here, I want to focus on the values that you hold at the deepest level. I like the model that suggests that we have three levels of consciousness: our conscious mind, our subconscious mind and our higher consciousness. I believe the higher consciousness is not in our heads, but in our hearts and is what connects us with the oneness of the universe; or the oneness that we can experience with all humanity. Values sit at a level above our subconscious beliefs — more aligned with our higher consciousness — and guide and steer our lives and our decision making. Since the decisions we make play a huge part in shaping our lives, our values also play a crucial role, since they drive our decisions.

Values are similar to beliefs in that we all have them and we all arrange them in a different order of priority. We also define our values by different criteria. For instance, a business associate and I may both greatly value integrity, but what that means to each of us might be remarkably different. I may think it shows less integrity if I get any benefits that other shareholders don't have access to. On the other hand, my associate may think it is ok to get *some* exclusive benefits if they are only small and not worth more than a certain amount. We reach different conclusions despite valuing the same thing because we were raised differently and have had different life experiences and different teachers along the way. Very rarely (if ever) in life are any two things seen in exactly the same way by two different sets of eyes.

Because values lay deep within us and are closely connected with who we are and how we live our lives, one of the most important things for us to realize when it comes to our happiness is that if we do something that is in conflict with our inner values (especially our highest priority inner values) we are likely to cause ourselves a deep level of pain or discomfort. To ensure that my decisions are in alignment with my deepest values and there are no inner conflicts raging within my psyche I developed a system I call 'Values-Based Decision Making'. Whether wars are raging outside or inside, they are both bad news. For us, and our happiness, inner conflict and inner misalignment is not good for our physical or emotional health.

The first step to applying the strategy of Values-Based Decision Making — which I will now refer to as VBDM, since I have not yet mastered touch-typing — is to list all of your values. Examples of the things that you highly value, and that are the guiding principles in your life, could include: integrity, optimum health and vitality, contributing to others, intimate relationships, adventure, friends and family, courage, money, personal growth, constant learning, power, meaningful work, spirituality, etc. Write or describe your values however you like.

Once you have written down all of your values, work out their order of priority to you today. Over time you may need to adjust the order as you amend what is more important to you on a deeper level. Remember that everything in life is a 'work in progress' and very much open to constant change.

Rewrite the list in priority order so that it is much easier for you to relate to and apply in the next part of the process — which, by the way, is super simple. The more complicated something is, the more possibility for something to go wrong. Hence I am a huge fan of keeping things simple in all areas of life.

Applying the VBDM tool is merely to be consciously aware of what your priorities are when it comes to making decisions in your life. Let me show you what I mean with a basic example. Suppose my top four values in priority order are:

1. Health and Vitality;

2. Intimate Relationship;

3. Business;

4. Money.

A financially lucrative business opportunity comes up that is mine for the taking. This opportunity would require me to move to England for 8 weeks in the middle of winter, without my partner, work 12-hour days 6 days a week, and stay in an apartment 1 hour away from the office. But the pay is awesome!

Using the VBDM tool, I compare the opportunity to my highest priorities and ask whether accepting it would positively or negatively impact on the things I value most dearly:

1. Would it affect my Health and Vitality? I would have less time to exercise and, given the season, being able to train outdoors, which I absolutely love to do, is unlikely. It might reduce the time I have to meditate and affect my access to healthy food. So it is a negative against my highest value.

2. Would it affect my Intimate Relationship? My partner and I had experienced something similar in the past and agreed that being apart for longer than 3 weeks would become unpleasant and disruptive to the relationship. Oops. Looks like a negative to this value, too.

3. Would it affect my Business? If I take the opportunity, it may jeopardize the success of the business I am currently running. While taking the opportunity will enhance some of my skills, those skills are not so necessary for running my current business. I count this as a neutral benefit.

4. Would it affect my Money situation? Absolutely. My bank balance would go right up and I could book that trip I have wanted to take for a couple of years. This is definitely a positive.

To tell the truth, this was similar to a real scenario I faced. In the end I saw that there were major conflicts with a few of my highest values, even though the money was great. I knew after using the Values-Based Decision Making tool that if I had been blinded by the money and taken the contract I would have arrived with an inner conflict. This would have affected the experience in an adverse way, possibly affecting my ability to perform the task well, and very likely would have affected my number 1 value: maintaining a high level of health and vitality.

A common example of what happens when we're not clear about our values and the order of priority in which we live by them is when someone decides that they want to lose weight or get fit. Let's name our case study Jeff. If Jeff is not clear about his values and does not understand where Health and Vitality sits in order of priority in his life, he will have a very hard time sticking with an exercise program. If for Jeff, Health and Vitality sits below Work, Entertainment and Money, there is a good chance that an activity related to his top 3 values will take precedence over a workout. Unless he is willing to bump Health and Vitality further up his list of priorities, for an exercise program to have priority in Jeff's decision making, he must figure out how losing weight and improving his health aligns with, for example:

1. Work — Jeff could identify reasons why working out will improve his work; for example, give him more energy, make him feel more vibrant, allow him to better handle stress.

2. Entertainment — Jeff realizes he can have fun in the fitness center by meeting new people, listening to the latest music, and taking classes he most enjoys.

3. Money — the more energy Jeff has the better the performance he can maintain at work, which might lead to a promotion, or saving money on medical bills.

Convincing yourself that a decision you made is the right one when you have feelings of inner conflict is a recipe for disaster and continued inner discomfort. You will feel on some level that you have sold out on yourself and even that you cannot trust yourself. To live a life of joy, it is extremely important to not only have noble values, but also to live by them through thick and thin. Otherwise your self-image and self-respect will be adversely affected and this will spill over into all other parts of your life.

Using the VBDM tool is an effective way to get clear of the 'noise' that other people's advice may create. In my experience the advice that people give often comes with strings attached to their own best interests. So it is good to hear the 'ideas' of others, but the greatest judge of what's best for you, when you are truly conscious of your values and courageous enough to listen to them, is yourself. A non-emotive tool like Values-Based Decision Making might be the perfect strategy to help you make your best decisions in life.

Summary

1. Clarify and understand your values and their order of priority in your life so the decisions you make always align with your deepest values and thus bring you inner peace (and inner health).

2. All values are not created equal between all people. The rules we attach to those values, and the order in which we prioritize them, make us different from each other. This is also why, in the end, we need to be comfortable with our own decisions. No one can know us as truly as we know ourselves.

3. When you make important decisions, use the Values-Based Decision Making tool to check how taking a certain decision will affect your values.

Happiness Strategies

1. Go to *www.theguidebooktohappiness.com* and download the free Values-Based Decision Making tool to help with future decision making.

2. Use the VBDM tool with a decision you are faced with at the moment.

3. Live your life in alignment with your highest values.

CHAPTER 12:

The human body (and mind) works best when it moves

There's no easy way out. If there were, I would have bought it.
And believe me, it would be one of my favorite things!
Oprah Winfrey, American media proprietor and philanthropist

One of the most effective ways to feel wonderful physically, mentally and emotionally, immediately and for a sustained period afterwards, is to engage in physical activity

Your body will love you for it

As Tal Ben-Shahar says, 'Not exercising is like taking a depressant'. Sonja Lyubomirsky, a scientist, renowned positive psychology researcher, and author of *The How of Happiness* says, 'No one in our society needs to be told that exercise is good for us. Whether you are overweight or have a chronic illness or are a slim couch potato, you've probably heard or read this dictum countless times throughout your life. But has anyone told you — indeed, guaranteed you — that regular physical activity will make you happier? I swear by it.'

The human body is truly amazing. Check out some of these statistics. In one day, our blood travels almost 20,000 km or 12,427 miles. In one year, our heart beats about 35 million times (unless you are hyperactive like me then it will be much more); and in a lifetime, our heart pumps *three super tankers* worth of blood throughout our body, that is, over 900 million liters or 250 million gallons. And that is just our heart!

We, as human beings, have been constructed in the same way regardless of where we live on planet Earth. We all (likely) have one heart, one brain, a couple of kidneys (or at least one), a liver, a circulatory system, a nervous system, etc. One of the many systems in the human body that plays an exceptionally important role in our health and therefore our happiness is the lymphatic system.

The lymphatic system plays a major role in the body's immune system and in the removal of waste and toxins from the body. The lymphatic system is essential to optimum health. One of the major differences between the lymphatic system and the circulatory system, which pumps our blood, is that the lymphatic system is dependent on the contraction of skeletal muscles, that is, the muscles that are connected to the bones, to function fully.

The contraction of skeletal muscles produces movement. To look at it from the other way round, in order to move the body, we need to contract our muscles. The more we move our bodies, the more this contraction occurs and the more the lymphatic system is able to do its job of cleansing the body of waste. No movement = poor circulation in the lymphatic system = waste and toxins not being effectively removed from the body = poor health.

This is a really important message for you to hear and understand. All of us living on planet Earth who belong to the species *homo sapiens* are designed to move our skeletal muscles regularly for the rest of our lives to be healthy and happy. Once you accept the fact that it is your lot in life — like brushing your teeth, washing your body, eating food — it's much easier to make it a part of your life and lifestyle. It's a done deal.

If you are not yet convinced about the absolute need for physical activity, here is some more good news. And who does not like getting good news?

The communities around the world were people live to the oldest age — from Abkhasia near Russia to the Hunza in the Himalayas, north of India, and Okinawa in Japan to Vilcabamba in Ecuador — have always maintained and continue to maintain a physically active lifestyle, including the elders. Whether it is walking, running, working in the fields, lifting heavy objects, hiking, or practicing yoga, regular physical activity is a common ingredient in people living healthily to 100 and beyond.

When we exercise we almost always (providing we haven't started hiking up Mount Everest after a 3-day 'Introduction to Bootcamp' program) feel great as a result because of the release of certain hormones. One of the most popular explanations for the psychological feelings of euphoria after exercise is the release of endorphins (actually beta-endorphins), naturally produced opiates in the brain, which contain morphine-like properties. So as well as euphoria, we also feel relief from pain. Pretty cool, hey! A legal, natural and healthy high. What more could we ask for?

Once upon a time — not that long ago really — people's main form of transport involved the use of the left and right legs; also known as walking. Even this very basic physical activity is no longer a daily activity. For some, it is not even a weekly activity. Many of us live in an automated world; we catch the lift rather than take the stairs, drive rather than walk to the shop, load the dishwasher rather than hand-wash the dirty dishes, click a button rather than raise the garage door by hand, email a colleague rather than walk to their desk, and the list goes on. We need to specifically seek out and perform physical activities to make up for not getting anywhere near enough of them in our current lifestyles. In the western world, we also tend to consume vastly higher numbers of calories than we need, so if we don't burn off the excess by being physically active, whether we like it or not, the body's 'standard operating procedure' is to store them as fat.

Where does the mind stand in relation to physical activity?

John Medina, PhD, author of *Brain Rules*, has found that 'exercisers outperform couch potatoes in tests that measure long-term memory, reasoning, attention, problem-solving, even so-called fluid-intelligence tasks.' I am sure you, like me, would also like to excel in at least a couple of things on that list. On aging, Dr Medina observed that 'one of the greatest predictors of successful aging was the presence or absence of a sedentary lifestyle.' Now given that 100% of the people reading this book are on the aging program, it might be time to switch into gear.

Dr Medina also states:

> "The role of exercise on mood is so pronounced that many psychiatrists have begun adding a regimen of physical activity to the normal course of therapy. In one experiment with depressed individuals, rigorous exercise was actually substituted for antidepressant medication. Even when compared against medical controls, the treatment outcomes were astonishingly successful. For both depression and anxiety, exercise is beneficial immediately and over the long-term."

John Ratey MD, author of *Spark: The Revolutionary New Science of Exercise and the Brain*, says that 'in addition to promoting better muscle tone and cardiovascular fitness, exercise is one of the best treatments we have for most psychiatric problems'. He also explains that 'exercise unleashes a cascade of neurochemicals and growth factors that serve to counter the affects of aging'.

One of the many reasons why exercising is so good for the mind (and slowing down aging) is that it increases the flow of oxygen to the brain. The brain accounts for only about 2% of our overall body weight, but uses over 20% of our oxygen intake. Exercising improves the cardiovascular system and increases the amount of blood and therefore oxygen that reaches the brain. And here's another interesting fact I came upon in my research. Apparently the brain can only fire off about 2% of its neurons at once, because it uses up so much energy to do so that firing off any more than that would exhaust us to the point of passing out. This made me realize that as well as engaging in physical activity, actively and effectively using the mind is also a good weight loss strategy.

As the medical professionals I have quoted above have found, physical activity is not only great for our body inside and out, it also has an enormous impact on our mental and emotional health.

Let's be clear

Understand at the deepest possible level the following:

1. Your happiness is directly affected positively or negatively by the amount of physical activity you do or don't do throughout your life.

2. The human body has been engineered in such a way that it requires regular daily movement of the body to perform its essential waste and toxin removal process. Physical activity is not an optional extra for good health and happiness; it is one of the main events.

3. Your brain functions more effectively as a result of physical activity. You even age more slowly if physical activity is an integral part of your life.

4. It is not so much about which physical activity you do, or how you do it, it is more about *doing something* physical every day. Ten minutes of walking is better than none. One game of hopscotch is better than none.

Now that we are clear about needing to undertake a physical activity program for life in order to achieve optimum health and happiness, I want to list a few other reasons why physical activity is so good for us:

*   Magic happens when we move our body. I have no scientific proof for this, you are just going to have to trust me!

*   It increases our lean muscle, which essentially means that we are burning more calories, even at rest.

*   It increases our energy levels. One of the reasons is that our level of energy

is directly affected by our emotional state. And we have already talked about those trippy chemicals that the body gives out for free when we exercise.

- To expand on the point above, the more energy we have, the shorter the timeframe we need to overcome the inevitable setbacks, traumas and surprises that happen in life. Our energy level can directly affect our emotional recovery time. In his book, *Healthy at 100*, John Robbins says on the topic:

  'What if there was a pill that would keep you fit and lean as you aged, while protecting your heart and bones? What if it was as good for your brain as for your body, if it made you stronger, more confident, less susceptible to depression? What if it improved your sleep, mood, and memory and reduced your risk of cancer, all while adding life to your years and years to your life? A great number of studies have found that exercise can provide all these benefits and more, even for people who begin late in life. We are learning that much of the physical decline that older people suffer stems not from age but from simple disuse.'

- Fred Gage, PhD, of the Salk Institute for Biological Studies, says, 'We now know that exercise helps generate new brain cells, even in the aging brain.'

- It improves heart health and circulation of blood throughout the body. It can also assist in reducing blood pressure.

- It can be a lot of fun if we choose activities that we enjoy doing. Who doesn't want more fun in their life?

- It can give us opportunities to experience social interaction with others, including with our pets. Many psychologists agree that loneliness is particularly harmful for our emotional and physical health. Social interaction positively affects our health and happiness and is a common characteristic of cultures that live healthily to older ages.

- It is an effective tool for managing stress. As already mentioned there are the chemical benefits, but also, by moving the body, we tend to change our focus from whatever is causing us stress onto the present moment, that is, sucking oxygen into our lungs to keep us moving.

- It is a key factor in having healthy bones. Many people erroneously think it makes bones more fragile, but on the contrary, exercise increases bone density. Bones, like muscles, need to be challenged to grow and strengthen. Essentially the body says, 'Phew, that weight was heavy. I had better start making more muscle fibres so I can handle this new challenge and be even more prepared for next time.' Or words to that effect. Bones are the same.

- It will help you look and feel great and people will be attracted and magnetized to you.

Summary

1. The body is designed such that the lymphatic system is dependent on movement of the skeletal muscles to perform its job of removing waste from the body, which is essential to our health. Physical activity is not an optional extra for good health and happiness; it is one of the main events.

2. Now that we no longer lead physical lives, we need to consciously seek out and perform regular physical activities.

3. Your happiness and health are joined at the hip. It is difficult, perhaps impossible, to experience a high level of happiness without good health. And one of the essential ingredients to good health is physical activity.

4. Without physical activity you will never reach your *full potential*. You won't earn the money, experience the depth of relationships, have the optimum health, fully explore the world, overcome setbacks as quickly, etc., etc., as you can when you are physically active.

5. The brain works more effectively as a result of physical activity, due to increased blood flow and oxygen.

6. Exercising slows down the aging process. This alone is enough for me!

Happiness Strategies

1. Write a list of all the physical activities that you enjoy doing, or would like to learn to do. Examples include horse riding, salsa dancing, hiking, adventure racing, bike riding, dancing around the office (one of my favorites), taking the dog for a walk, roller blading, ice skating, rock climbing, weight lifting, boxing, martial arts, and practicing yoga and pilates.

2. Schedule the days and times that you will do these activities each week. Do at least 3 physical activities a week, 4 if you want a silver star, or 5 if you want a gold star!

3. Do some physical activity today, even if it is just walking on the spot in the lounge room during an advertisement break on the television. Did you know that Nelson Mandela, when he was in his 5 m² (54 ft²) prison cell on Robben Island for 18 years, walked on the spot for up to an hour most days to stay fit and healthy? Do you have any excuses now?

4. Seek the help of a professional or others if you need help getting the best out of your physical activities.

CHAPTER 13:

E + R = O

How you choose to respond each moment to the movie of life determines how you see the next frame, and the next, and eventually how you feel when the movie ends.

Doc Childre, American founder of Heartmath Institute

I came across this simple equation when reading *The Success Principles* by Jack Canfield, co-founder of the *Chicken Soup* for the Soul series. In the book, Canfield attributes its origins to Dr Robert Resnick, a psychotherapist from California. I thank the clever mind behind the equation, especially for its being so simple.

The full equation reads like this:

An Event (**E**) plus your Response to that event (**R**) will determine the final Outcome (**O**).

Just let that statement sink in for a while. The *event*, plus your response to it is what will determine the final *outcome*. The event itself does not determine the outcome. First it must filter through us. It implies that we are the ones responsible for the outcomes we see in life. That is a really big pill to swallow for many people, who will continue to say that the external environment or other people are responsible for their life and they cannot change that 'fact'.

For some people, life will always happen to them, and it will be either *good* or *bad* as determined by the external event. The challenge with that way of living is that you have very little control in your life. We have evolved so much further from ancient civilizations that believed that everything that happened to them was the will of the gods or due to some other external force. Psychology and neuroscience now show us that we can choose a response and even choose the meaning that we give to an event.

We become a filter through which life passes, and it is the way we filter, that is, interpret life that makes its events empowering or disempowering. Many of the most successful people on the planet experienced an apparently negative situation or event in life, such as extreme poverty, losing their parents at an early age, or having their business fail, but went on to create great success.

In hindsight the situation or event could be viewed as positive. While it may not necessarily be positive in and of itself, the difference lies in the interpretation of what happened. Chances are that you too could name an event in your past that you initially thought was a complete disaster, but in the end, led to something great.

E + R = O is amazingly relevant and powerful. Buddhist and other philosophers have been saying for centuries, 'there is no meaning to an event, except for the meaning that we give it'. It is by our response that we decide whether something will be a learning event, a life-destroying event, a neutral event, a sad event, a joyous event, etc. It is the meaning that we give something that will also determine what chemicals — otherwise known as emotions — our brain causes the body to release. Choose a positive label and you will generate a feel-good chemical cocktail. And, you guessed it: choose a negative label and you flood your body with a rush of feel-really-awful chemicals.

Let me give you an example. I am writing this in Bali, which is world famous for having some of the best surfing waves on the planet, so I'll use the beach for my setting. Two people standing next to each other on the beach are looking at exactly the same big, rolling wave crashing on the shore. Since they are the same height and only 1 metre separates them, their visual perspective of the wave is almost identical. The person on the left sees the wave as a thing of absolute beauty, challenge and fun. It causes all of these feel-good chemicals to flow through her body, which makes her feel energized, connected and grateful to be alive.

The person on the right has absolute fear written all over his face. He sees the wave as a threat to his life, which immediately causes his body to react with a fight or flight response. He now feels tension in his stomach, his heart is beating more rapidly, he is breathing more shallowly, and he feels disconnected.

They were both looking at the same wave so what made one person feel joy (and a chemical high) and the other feel pure fear (and activate the fight or flight response)? It was not the wave itself; it was the *meaning* that each gave the wave. Their response to the wave crashing on the shore (the *event*) caused the emotions and the physical expression of those emotions (the feel-good or feel-bad *outcome*).

How about another example? A couple are in an intimate relationship for 5 years until one of them decides categorically, no-questions-asked, no-room-for-discussion, that they want to separate. The person that has been 'left behind, dumped, side-swiped, etc.' has several choices as to how they can RESPOND and I want you to consider how different the OUTCOME might be in each case:

1. They scream, yell, and wail about how unfair life is and then go on a drinking binge for the next 2 years, while complaining to everyone they meet that life is so unfair.

2. They scream, yell, and wail about how unfair life is and then go down to the pub, drink themselves senseless, then decide the next day to move out to their friend's place and think through their next move.

3. They scream, yell, and wail about how unfair life is and then go for a

long walk. When they return they pack up some things and go to stay at their friend's place. Over the next few days they reflect on what was great about the relationship, what was not great, what they learned out of the relationship and how they are going to move forward.

4.   They scream, yell, and wail about how unfair life is and then think, 'I am actually glad that my partner had the courage to leave what was essentially a loveless relationship and now we can both move on with our lives.'

Put simply, better responses lead to better outcomes. And regardless of what we may have led ourselves to believe, we *always* have a choice as to how we will respond in any situation. The choice may be very hard to make, but we still have a choice.

Responding vs. reacting

The words 'reacting' and 'responding' are at times interchangeable. However, I think of reacting as what an animal does, and responding as what us homo sapiens *have the ability to do*. Reacting is a result of using the reptilian part of our mind (the lower and the oldest part of our brain), which is limited to fight, flight, or freeze; whereas responding uses our highly developed prefrontal lobe (the front part of the neocortex, the upper and most evolved part of our brain which keeps us at the top of the food chain).

When you *respond*, the process is more like this:

1.   The event happens.

2.   You observe the event.

3.   You breathe, which sends oxygen to the brain.

4.   You consciously think, which uses the more developed parts of your brain that you cannot access in fight or flight mode.

5.   You make a conscious decision.

6.   You take action.

7. Your created outcome is realized.

Very infrequently, in our modern world, are we in life-threatening situations, which require us to launch into a full-blown sprint or to start filling the meeting room with upper cuts, slaps or sucker punches. In almost all situations we have the time to pause, breathe, think, and then respond; rather than just reacting like a startled lizard. Don't get me wrong. Lizards are cool. I just think that we are all capable of so much more than our four-legged friends.

'Responding' is especially important when it comes to relationships. I like to teach people to take a breath (or 5) before *consciously responding* to a comment by someone. Especially to someone that is close to us. This short time taken to think of an appropriate response (or none), can make a huge difference to the quality of our relationships and connections with others. Also, given that the brain uses about 20% of the oxygen that comes into the body, the extra breathing will help you relax the body and energize the mind, so you will also be at your smartest.

Summary

E + R = O

1. It is our *Response* to any given *Event* that determines what the final *Outcome* will be.

2. We are free to decide what meaning we give to situations and then what behavior (or actions) we carry out. It is that meaning and that behavior which will have the greatest bearing on the end result.

3. Countless success stories have come from what appeared to be negative events or situations. Philosophers through the ages have said that our greatest mistakes or setbacks can be our greatest teachers.

4. Choose to 'respond' to all situations, as opposed to habitually 'react'. Reacting may have been valid when you were 8 years old, but now that

you are an adult, you can choose a better option.

Happiness Strategies

1. Know that you are in control and can make conscious decisions (by thinking with the neocortex) as to what meaning you are going to give, or take, from a particular event.

2. Always breathe before you respond. It will make you smarter. Practically and scientifically.

3. I acknowledge that it is sometimes hard to change our habitual thinking. That is why it is important to bring even more consciousness (thinking) to our responses. The more you notice your pattern of thinking (or labelling), the easier it will be to change. And if you need help with changing your thinking, there is support available. You can take up the WorldsBIGGESTGym™ *30-Day Happiness Challenge*, or see a Life Coach or NLP Practitioner. Changing your thinking is the key to changing your life.

CHAPTER 14:
Liquid gold for the body

Pure water is the world's first and foremost medicine.
Slovakian proverb

Let's get right into the facts here. Our bodies mainly consist of water, good old H_2O. Since we lose fluid through urination, and through our bowels, skin, and breath, what should we be ingesting into our body on a regular basis? If you said beer, I am going to have to ask you to march yourself to the principal's office for a good old-fashioned dose of corporal punishment.

The literature on the exact water content of our body seems to be changing a little depending on who is providing the information but as a general guide the human body is made up of about 75% water and the brain is made up of slightly more, up to 80%. Water is essential to keeping us alive and for the healthy functioning of our body, and even more so, our brain, which determines our success.

So how does water and water consumption relate to our happiness? Well to highlight the relationship that water, or as I like to call it, liquid gold, has to our level of happiness, below is a list of physical scenarios. Ask yourself whether they would make you happy or unhappy:

- An inability to go to the bathroom because you are constipated.

- A headache at the front of your head.

- A lack of energy.

- Feeling hungry and being at least 10 blocks from the nearest cafeteria.

- Feeling bloated because the body thinks there is a shortage of water and has retained it.

- Dry or tired-looking skin.

Water is the most important nutrient we can feed the body. We can go without food for weeks, but if we go without water for even a day we become dehydrated and within a few days we die, simple as that. Water is imperative for healthy muscle function, kidney function, waste removal and other essential bodily functions.

There is a lot of conflicting information on how much water is best for us to consume. The suggestion that we should drink 8 glasses of water a day is just that: A suggestion. One calculation is to divide your weight by 2 if you are using pounds and ounces; for example, if you weigh 150 pounds then consume 75 ounces of water per day, or divide your weight by 30 if you are using kilograms and litres; for example, if you weigh 70kg then consume over 2 litres of water per day. I always like to round up and add a little more to allow for exercise, a warm climate, an artificial environment such as air conditioning or heating, and in 99% of cases if you drink more than you need you will just excrete the excess. There have been rare cases of people over-consuming water and dying or becoming seriously ill as a result, but these usually relate to people doing excessive exercise and not having sufficient electrolytes or sodium in their bodies (which is further diluted by large intakes of water). The chance of you or the vast majority of the population drinking too much water to the point that it becomes a health risk is very low.

If you wish to lose weight or are conscious of your weight it is especially important to ensure that you are drinking appropriate amounts of water. If you do not drink enough water, your body may think there is a drought and retain water in your body, which causes bloating. It is also the best fluid to drink if you want to lose weight, as it contains no calories. And quite often when you think you are hungry you may find that it is more a case of mild dehydration. Therefore if you are feeling hungry the first thing you should reach for (instead of that chocolate bar) is a glass of water. Drink first and chances are your hunger pangs will be significantly reduced. If not, reach PAST the chocolate bar and help yourself to some raw organic almonds to snack on. The good fats inside the almonds will help you feel satiated and your desire for the calorie-rich nutrient-poor snack will decrease. Are you feeling hungry about now? Quickly. Drink that glass of water!

It has been suggested that a large percentage of the global population is actually dehydrated on a consistent and daily basis, not only due to insufficient water consumption but also the over-consumption of diuretics such as coffee and other caffeinated drinks, and alcohol. Diuretics actually increase the excretion of fluids from the body and decrease the absorption of fluids into the cells, which makes someone who consumes too little water more susceptible to dehydration.

Drinking water is such a simple happiness strategy. If you are feeling low in energy at any time of the day, the first thing you want to do is drink a full glass of water. This will generally give you an energy boost. Also when you are working to be your most creative and solution-oriented problem solver (which is a key ingredient to success in life), make sure you are fully hydrated and be inclined to drink a little more water, even if this means that you take an extra trip or two to the WC. The extra water (not coffee, soft drinks or sodas) will make you more vibrant and stimulated.

Before we finish up, a short word on coffee, which happens to be the second highest commodity traded after crude oil since over 2 billion cups of coffee are consumed around the world every day! If you have no more than 2 standard (8 ounce or 250ml) cups of coffee a day, then you are not causing any problems for your body. But going above 2 cups a day you may actually start to go backwards. Over 2 cups a day is about the stage where the excess caffeine (which is acidic) starts to leech a few of the key micronutrients from your body, in particular calcium, which comes from your bones and is trying to neutralize the acidic nature of the caffeine. This applies to all caffeinated drinks including teas, soft drinks and sodas.

Summary

1. Drink plenty of water each day. Let it be the main fluid that you put into your body. It is what the body craves and needs to survive, and also comes with zero calories.

2. If you are tired or want to do your best thinking, make sure you are fully hydrated. If unsure, then drink a glass of water for good measure.

3. Drinking too much coffee, tea, or caffeinated drinks (more than 2 cups a day as a guide) may cause your body to excrete water and leech calcium out of your bones.

4. I was just reflecting on how much water I consume when I am writing. It is somewhere between 4 and 6 litres (or 16 to 24, 12-ounce glasses) a day. I think more clearly and am more creative when I am fully hydrated. I also snack on almonds, which are great brain food. Plus I do not eat heavily; the energy required to digest a big meal is significant; thus I have more energy for thinking, creating and two-finger typing on my keyboard!

Happiness Strategies

1. Drink more water every day (at least 8 to 10 glasses a day).

2. Drink water before a meal, which will generally cause you to eat less.

3. Stop at 2 cups of coffee (8 ounces or 250mls) or caffeinated drinks a day.

CHAPTER 15:

Rest up or fall down

What is without periods of rest will not endure.
Ovid, Roman poet

One of my favourite fiction books is Robert Ludlum's *The Bourne Identity*. At certain moments in the book, the protagonist, Jason Bourne, is reminded of a lesson he learned during his training, 'Rest is a weapon.' Although this sounds like an oxymoron, there is definitely truth in the statement. When you are tired and have low energy, how effective a weapon are you to deal with life's daily challenges? Instead of a samurai sword, I am picturing a wilted stick of 7-day old celery.

In *The Power of Full Engagement* by Jim Loehr and Tony Schwartz, the authors talk about what differentiates the world's top-level tennis players from players on the next level down. They found that it was not necessarily their skill, or style, or ability to read the game. One of the key differentiators was the ability to lower the heart rate after each point was played. As soon as a point was over, whether it was won or lost, the top players would relax their bodies enough to significantly lower the beats per minute of their heart, giving their bodies a mini-rest. Meanwhile, their opponent's heart rate is beating at a constant, high rate, which leads his or her body to exhaust quicker.

Resting like this between each point meant the top players could sustain a higher level of effort for a much longer period of time. Loehr and Schwartz also say that 'managing energy, not time, is the key to high performance and personal renewal'.

As already discussed, the energy we have available to play the game of life is directly affected by the energy that comes in and the energy that we expend. One of the best ways to manage our energy reserves is to ensure we get effective and adequate rest. And I am not just talking about the sleep we get each night. As with the top-level tennis players studied, a mini-rest can make the difference between high and medium-level achievement.

Loehr and Schwartz suggest that we are more productive if we take mini-breaks every 90 to 120 minutes, rather than putting in a mammoth effort and working like an 18th century coal miner for 12 hours straight. They contend that our powers of recall and effectiveness are improved as a result of taking regular breaks. It is in these mini-breaks that we solidify ideas, think of new ideas and give the brain some much-needed rest, all of which leads to a better end result.

No longer do you need to feel guilty for taking mini-breaks throughout the day. In fact, if your boss asks why you take a short stroll outside the office every 90 minutes or so, you can respond by saying, 'Studies have shown that the level of productivity that one can achieve is actually increased by taking a mini-break every 90 minutes. But I am sure you already know that.' *Caveat: if you do respond this way, you may end up shopping for a new employer.*

Some of the most effective mini-breaks include taking a short stroll (in nature if possible), having a brief talk (and stroll) with a work colleague, doing a conscious breathing exercise for 5 minutes, doing some light physical stretches, writing down a list of things you are grateful for as you look out over the horizon of possibility, or doing a random act of kindness for a colleague, client, or even a stranger. Checking social media websites or surfing the internet is generally not considered restful because your mind is still being stimulated and your attention is being pulled in different directions.

The answer to how much sleep we need each day to perform at our optimum, have the highest levels of energy and be as happy as possible can range widely. Most studies suggest the optimum amount of sleep is somewhere between 7.5 to 9 hours for an adult. This is obviously higher for babies, who need 12 to 18 hours, and children, who need 8.5 to 12 hours, depending on age.

Although research suggests that there is a small percentage of the population that are genetically wired to need fewer than 7 hours' sleep a day, for most people, this would have an adverse effect. There is limited evidence to suggest that sleeping longer than 9 hours a day (for adults) makes any measurable increase to energy levels and health. When someone feels they need 12 hours' sleep a day, it might be time to reassess all aspects of their life and lifestyle to establish what might be causing the excessive loss of energy. Obviously if someone is recovering from a health issue, operation, or illness, the body will require a lot more rest time to fully recover.

The *quality* of our sleep is also important and can have a bigger impact on our waking hours than the total number of hours we slept. At the risk of actually sending you to sleep, here are some facts.

When we sleep, the brain manages to conduct trillions of biological functions within the body related to repair, elimination and digestion, just to name a few. There are also two main types of sleep and they occur in a cyclical pattern lasting about 90 minutes each and happening about 4 to 6 times each night:

1. **Non-REM** sleep (3 stages): transition to sleep (first 5 minutes), light sleep (next 10 to 25 minutes), and deep sleep.

2. **REM** (rapid eye movement) sleep: happens about 70 to 90 minutes after you fall asleep, and can result in your most interesting dreams, the ones where, if you're lucky, you are a super star, loved by the masses and catch the man or woman of your dreams, so to speak, as they fall into your arms.

In very simplistic terms Non-REM Deep Sleep rejuvenates the body and REM Sleep rejuvenates the mind. Therefore, it is very important for the body and mind to have enough time, and enough cycle time, to get adequate non-REM deep sleep as well as REM sleep. Not getting enough sleep, that is, fewer than 7 hours, is likely to adversely affect most people. The adverse effects could include a loss of concentration, creativity, physical vitality and mental sharpness, which can lead to accidents like telling your boss or your partner what you were really thinking when they asked. Lack of sleep is definitely bad for (your) business.

If you think you are doing perfectly fine on 5 to 6 hours' sleep a night it might be time to do an experiment on yourself. Try a 7-day period where you get 7.5 hours of sleep each night. See if there are any noticeable differences. Do you have more energy? Are you more productive? Are you more creative? Have you pissed off the people around you less than usual? Think about how much your life would improve if your daily energy was improved by just 10%. This is the impact that getting the right amount of sleep could make.

Now I want to talk about my favorite type of rest, macro-breaks. Macro-breaks make a huge impact on our life and happiness over the long term. They are rests we take weekly, monthly, quarterly, yearly, five-yearly and decadely (yep, I made up that word) and are where fun, happiness and rejuvenation all come together in a beautiful tribal dance to make a remarkably positive difference in your life and in the lives of those around you.

The following recommendations are based on science, personal experience, or the thought, 'what an awesome idea!':

1. **Weekly**. We need one day off each week from that thing we call 'work'. Even if we love what we do, there are creative and productivity benefits from stopping once a week. If you dig around on the internet you will also find the term 'circaseptan rhythm' which relates to a 7-day natural body cycle. Some research suggests that we have a natural 7-day rhythmic

cycle similar to our daily circadian rhythms. One article even suggested that during the French Revolution an attempt was made to instil a 10-day (metric) working week, to ill effect, before the 7-day cycle was restored. Regardless of its history, the benefits of having at least one day off, during which no work is done, in a 7-day cycle can include increased productivity and creativity, deeper relationships, and better health and happiness.

2. **Monthly.** I am a big believer and fan of a monthly break where you take out 3 to 4 days (or more) to rest and rejuvenate. This is the time to work on relationships. To do things that you find enjoyable. To connect with nature. To unplug from mobile phones, emails, text messages, alarm clocks and any other technology that has you wired in with no down time and beeps and buzzes to distract you. Have you ever thought about the term 'alarm clock'? It might just be me, but 'alarm' doesn't sound like fun to me. Disconnect for a few days every month and your happiness muscles will thank you for it.

3. **Quarterly**. How do you think you would feel if you took 5 to 10 days off every 3 months? You could gather your partner, family or friends and embark on an activity or adventure together with those people that are most important to you. Or even take a break that encourages and enables you to meet new people. How good would that be for your overall happiness?

4. **Yearly.** I suspect I don't need to convince anyone of the benefits of taking an extended vacation, going on a retreat, or having an adventure every year. It is definitely possible. You just need to plan for it and get creative if you are in a work situation where your days off, or vacation time, are limited. You might need to save more money over the year and take unpaid vacation. You might need to mix in work and rest, such as work for 4 days and explore for 3 days (or preferably the other way around). Know that taking a reasonable yearly break, to somewhere new, interesting and exciting, will rejuvenate you and is also likely to make you more productive and effective when you return to work. Plus it is likely to enhance your relationships, which form a major part of your life's happiness. New sensory inputs and experiences lead to a growth of neuron activity within

the brain. So do what you have to do, but organize a good trip, vacation or adventure each year. These days, with budget airlines, countries with lower costs of living, and access to all corners of the globe, it has become easier than it ever was.

5. **Sabbaticals.** These are generally thought of as what professors or other creative types traditionally take every 7 years. But why can't it apply to you? Would you like to travel the globe or your country for 3 months, 6 months or 12 months? Or work on that charity project for an extended period of time? If you are nodding your head right now, know that it is possible and much easier than it has ever been. First, set your goal destination, then make the plans, one of which might involve saving 10% or more of your salary each month to put towards your adventure. I have traveled all over the world using this method. I would work for 5 years, then travel abroad for 1 year. I chose to start a family later in life so I could do this, but I once met an Australian couple with two daughters aged 10 and 12 years on the Inca Trail to Machu Picchu in Peru who were traveling the world for 1 year as a family. Can you imagine the education the children received on that trip? I can just picture one of their teachers making a point about a foreign culture and one of the girls saying, 'Actually, Miss, when I traveled through that country, I found it to be rather different to that ...'

If you have any misgivings about the importance of taking scheduled breaks throughout your life, think about this. How many people on their death bed would you assume whisper with regret, 'Oh I wish I had worked more days in my life and taken a lot less time off to have fun and seek adventure.' I have not conducted research on the regularity of this statement being heard, but I confidently guess that the answer is not one.

Summary

1. Taking quality mini-breaks throughout the day every 90 to 120 minutes will improve your productivity and effectiveness.

2. Most adults (research suggests around 80%) need between 7.5 and 9 hours sleep a day to be most effective and to avoid the trouble a tired, runaway mouth can cause.

3. The *quality* of our sleep is as important, or more important, as the number of hours' sleep we get. Deep uninterrupted sleep is best. This means that mobile phones are turned off or set to silent mode unless the fate of the world rests on your shoulders.

4. Just like we need mini-breaks, we also need macro-breaks. Weekly, monthly, quarterly, yearly, and even every 5 to 10 years. These are times to dedicate to family relationships or friendships, personal health and development, enjoying life, and boosting feelings of happiness and purpose in your life.

Happiness Strategies

1. Turn your mobile phone off or set it to silent mode overnight.

2. Aim to sleep at least 7.5 hours a night. If you generally sleep fewer than 7.5 hours, conduct a 7-day trial to see if 7.5 to 9 hours' sleep makes a difference to your energy and concentration levels.

3. Block out the following on your calendar:

    a. At least one day off a week.

    b. At least 2 to 4 consecutive days' break every month (where you do ZERO work). That includes no emails!

    c. An extended period of 5 to 10 days off work every 3 to 4 months. Get away somewhere. It does not have to be expensive. Go back to basics and camp.

    d. A yearly break, vacation or retreat. Ideally, find something that is a combination of relaxation, rejuvenation and personal growth.

Recommended reference material contains some ideas.

e. If you are not sleeping well then seek the help of a sleep expert. A sleep expert is likely to know more than your general practitioner and will find solutions and strategies that do not depend on pharmaceuticals but add to or change your lifestyle. Sleep has a huge impact on our waking hours, so doing it as effectively as possible is well worth it.

CHAPTER 16:

Who are your teachers?

The most important day I remember in all my life is the one on which my teacher, Anne Sullivan, came to me. I am filled with wonder when I consider the immeasurable contrasts between the two lives, which it connects. It was the third of March 1887, three months before I was seven years old

Helen Keller, American author, political activist and lecturer

What do you think are your chances of being financially abundant in life if the person who was teaching you did not know how to be so themselves? While they may have done their best, most of what they taught you may have been assumed, speculated, hypothesized, even fabricated. Over time, perhaps you learned to mistrust your own intuition and to listen to advice from people who had no idea what they were talking about, but who sounded confident in their delivery. It makes me laugh (which is much better than crying) when I think of the stupid things I have done because I did not believe in myself, or I mistakenly assumed that the person who spoke the loudest knew better than I did; when I allowed their voice to overcome my own intuition. We all know someone, or have been that person ourselves, who has made a really bad decision based on poor advice.

This chapter is all about trusting yourself, doing more research on who is providing you advice, and surrounding yourself with people that have the physical results to show that the advice they are giving is sound. While it is as simple as not doing or entering into business, or forming a close relationship, with someone we do not trust, knowing that doesn't stop us from sometimes falling into the trap of listening to others and ignoring our own niggling misgivings. Different studies suggest that we often decide if we trust someone within the first 10 seconds of meeting them. If you have a 'feeling' that you do not trust someone fully, then you might want to listen to that feeling, and leave your checkbook in your pocket, or your heart in your chest cavity.

Our teachers are those closest to us in our life, from our first teachers, our parents, to our colleagues and friends. So many people from all aspects of our lives offer us advice on how to live, whether or not we ask for it. It is important to be alert to the quality of the advice and decide how much weight it deserves to be given, if any at all.

Jim Rohn, an American motivational speaker and personal development expert, is credited for saying that 'you are the average of the five people you spend most time with'. Specifically, Rohn suggests that we earn the average income of what those five people earn, and adopt the average of their levels of happiness, optimism and integrity, too. We are much more affected by our environment than we may realize. Paramahansa Yogananda, mentioned in Chapter 4 in relation to Daily Rituals, also cautioned, 'the environment is stronger than the willpower'.

If you spend time with criminals, you are much more likely to commit illegal or unethical acts yourself. If you surround yourself with people that are always complaining, you find yourself joining in until complaining becomes a habit or part of your personality. To build rapport with the people around us, or to be liked, or to avoid criticism, we tend to conform to the group mentality. This is also referred to in psychology and leadership literature as 'group think', and I am sure you know the power of the group.

If the power of the group has the ability to change you to the average of the group, then I highly recommend joining the happiest group. Instead of joining the group of complainers, join the group of optimists. Instead of joining the financial strugglers (who blame the world, government and share markets for their situation), spend time with the ethical millionaires. Instead of hanging out with gang members, hang out with people that are hungry for an education and to better their station in life. Remember, it is up to us whom we choose to spend most of our time with.

The last line may have prompted you to think, 'Sure, I can choose my friends, but I can't choose my family.' Of course that's true, but you can choose how long you spend with them. In some cases it might be the best thing for your family when you tell them the reason you do not spend more time with them — it might cause them to think and change themselves, if they value your company. Protecting their precious time is one of the key traits of highly successful people. They know they only have 24 hours in the day (as we all do) and are thus very selective of even the minutes they give out to people, projects and opportunities. If you want to be a happy and healthy high achiever, start protecting your time and be very conscious of to whom and how you allocate your time.

When seeking or acting on advice be very clear about who it is that is giving you the advice. Ask them questions to ascertain their credibility. These days, it is easy to research people via various social media websites and blogs. There is no excuse for following bad advice because you did not know any better.

Remember that another powerful person who is able to provide cutting-edge, relevant advice is YOU! Too often we look everywhere else for the right advice, or seek out others to guide us, when one of the best guides is our own intuition. Our intuition or subconscious mind conducts the process of 'thin slicing' (a term used by Malcolm Gladwell in his book *Blink*), which is the ability to pick things up in less than a heartbeat about a person or situation, based on thousands of factors that our mind has immediate access to. This is how a police officer 'just knows' that something is not right about that person walking across the park 100 yards away. Their conscious mind takes a while to catch up to what their subconscious mind has already deduced. Learn to connect with and trust this inner intuition.

One of the best decisions I ever made was to invest in myself, and it took my life in a whole new direction. I had been consulting to the Olympic Games and 2006 Asia Games for a number of years and saved up a decent amount of money. In 2007, after doing some research and a quick course on financial investing I invested the bulk of my money in managed funds. Then, in October 2008, my shares, along with those of a lot of other people all over the world, took a complete nosedive and I lost a bunch of my hard-earned cash.

Not one to shed tears, I carefully assessed the situation and my actions during this time to learn as much as possible, and in 2010 I invested the remaining money in my company, WorldsBIGGESTGym™. I could not have been happier with this decision, mostly because of the control and autonomy it gave me over my financial future. In psychology it is commonly agreed that a sense of autonomy is one of the key attributes to good emotional health. Now before you rush out and cash in your shares to start up your own company, make sure you do your own due diligence. The decision I made was right for me at the time and would probably not have worked 5 years prior because I was not yet ready.

I want to tell you another personal story, about listening to one of the greatest teachers you have access to — you. In 2008, I had the opportunity to get involved in a project in Bali. The outline on paper was excellent. The opportunities for return on investment were great. The ability to expand the business appeared healthy. Coming from the approach of 'I've never done anything like this before', it looked like a fabulous deal. However, only a little way into the initial discussions I had an uncomfortable feeling in the base of my stomach when I thought about one of the key players involved in the project. But I chose to suppress and ignore this strong intuitive advice coming from the teacher within. As a result of not listening to this pertinent advice (nor seeking the advice of someone who had already been through something similar), the project was an emotional rollercoaster, costing me far too much wasted energy and excessive stress.

Summary

1. Be very selective about who you spend the majority of your time with. You become the average of the five people you spend the most time with and, as Mr Yogananda said, 'the environment is stronger than the willpower'. One of the reasons for this is that your environment slowly seeps into you unawares. Often, you don't put up any defences until it is too late and the change has already been made. Hence, one of the most powerful ways to consciously bring about change is to change your environment for one that is super positive and optimistic.

2. Don't take financial advice from someone that is in debt and has no money in the bank and no assets just because they regularly read the *Financial Times*. Results matter.

3. Tap into your intuition. Trust your own deep feelings when it comes to decision making. Get used to doing the intellectual checks and balances and then check in on how you 'feel' about the whole decision. Warren Buffet, one of the richest men in the world, has an uncanny knack of looking at undervalued businesses and not only intellectually, but intuitively, deciding if they are a good deal.

Happiness Strategies

1. Observe who you spend most of your time with. You do not have to stay in contact with a childhood friend if you don't enjoy and feel drained of energy after spending time with them.

2. Limit time with family members who don't support your direction or philosophies in life. It doesn't mean your love for them diminishes, but as I tell my family, 'I love you, it's just that I love living in the countryside,

in a place where I cannot speak the language and I can wear shorts all year round.'

3. Tune in to your intuition. With any decisions you make over the next week, ask yourself, 'How do I feel about this?' Really listen to the message you are given.

CHAPTER 17:

Your words are either helping or hindering you

If you wish to know the mind of a man, listen to his words.
Chinese proverb

Have you ever said anything that you wished had never taken form inside your mind and, more importantly, had never left the confines of your mouth? How many thousands of times have we all done this? I estimate my latest count (though it is down to a trickle now) to be 1,425.5 — I added the 0.5 to account for one comment I caught half way; it came out as a garbled, unintelligible mumble, making me look like a mere weirdo as opposed to a complete and utter fool. I'd choose the weirdo any day over the fool.

Alternatively, how many times have you been on the receiving end of inappropriate or downright rude comments? One of my best friends once told me that I was the most annoying person in the whole world, to which I responded by feeling flattered. Over time, I have learned to make words, any words, work for me. Being able to transform negative comments from a person (and we all hear plenty over our lifetime) and turn them into positive compliments is a useful skill to master in your quest for more happiness. I have refined the art of turning criticisms into compliments and it's something I suggest you get good at too. Here are some examples:

1. 'You are a complete weirdo!' becomes 'You are so different and special.'

2. 'I want to slap you in the face' becomes 'You stir up my emotions so much.'

3. 'Why don't you get lost' becomes 'I am so overwhelmed by your personal power that I can hardly breathe, so I need you to step away for a while.'

4. 'You are really crap at doing that' becomes 'You stand out so much from the crowd that I just had to say something to you.'

This is an effective strategy if you tend to be overly sensitive to the comments of others. If someone says something negative to you, play this game of *Critiques to Compliments* and you'll feel better about yourself. It has worked for me for years, bringing me safely through the days when I was an absolute pain in the butt and attracted a *lot* more criticism than compliments. Also keep in mind that most people's adverse reactions are generally more about their own issues than about you. For instance, someone may tell me, 'Don't be so unrealistic. You are far too optimistic and deny reality'. The issue is probably not about my being optimistic, but more about that person's fear of daring to believe in the possibility of a better outcome because they have conditioned themselves to always see the negative in things.

Remember also that the greatest people to ever walk the earth (Jesus, Mohammed, Gandhi, Mother Teresa, Buddha, Martin Luther King Jnr, Nelson Mandela, etc.) were not liked by everyone. They had not only words but stones or worse thrown at them. If these luminary greats couldn't manage being loved by everyone, how are we to do it? You are not going to be the first person in the history of human existence to be loved by everyone. So stop getting upset when someone doesn't like you. Did they throw rocks at you? Nail you to a cross? Throw you in prison for challenging the norm? No? Then put that smile back on your face and remind yourself how AWESOME you really are!

A number of years ago I studied and was trained in Neuro Linguistic Programming or NLP as it is more commonly referred to. The area I was most intrigued by was the 'L' component. Linguistics relates to the language we use and the way in which we use it — both internally and externally. The deeper study of NLP delves into the realm of hypnosis, which is all about the use of words and how they are delivered. The results achieved are quite remarkable and border on magical. And just to debunk the mystery surrounding hypnosis, in a very general sense, it is using techniques and language to bypass the (critical) conscious mind and gain access to the VERY POWERFUL subconscious mind.

I now understand that the words coming from our mouths are a direct reflection of our thoughts and the beliefs that we hold about everything in our world. If the words leaving my mouth were not helping me achieve the results that I desired, I learned to reflect on the thought process and beliefs I had held that led me to speak such words. I had to become very conscious of the language I was using within my own mind. Was I using positive or negative language? Were my words empowering or disempowering me? Was I beating myself up or was I inspiring myself to do better? What did this dialogue look like in my mind? If I could change, or be more conscious of the dialogue in my mind, then the words that slipped past my lips were likely to create more of what I wanted in life, as opposed to what I didn't want.

This is what I came to realize and what I believe is most valuable:

1. Just because you are having a conversation in your mind and it is not released in the spoken form does not mean the language inside your mind will not affect you. In fact, it is likely to affect you more because we all have a bad habit of playing the stuff in our mind on a theater-quality Digital Surround Sound system on a loop recording! Our thoughts also cause the production of either a helpful or hindering chemical cocktail that is released into our body, which will determine our emotions and behavior. A good strategy to use is to talk to yourself as you would talk to a young child who you dearly love. If that young child made a mistake, would you abuse her, call her stupid, and go on and on and on about it? I don't think so. Now talk to yourself in the same way you would talk to that child you love dearly.

2. You can attribute a 'negative', 'neutral' or 'positive' emotional response to almost any word. It is up to you to choose words that cause you to experience a more positive and empowering emotion. For example, which word of the two listed below in each example do you think will bring out your best, and create more positive, more empowering and fewer negative feelings in your body?

    a. Problem or Challenge.

    b. Confused or Suffocated.

    c. Unsure or Struggling.

    d. Regrouping or Ruined.

    e. Failure or Feedback.

    f. Different or Hated.

3. The 'negative' options above are what I call 'emotive language'. These words are useful for writing a best-selling dramatic novel, but draining when you want to live an enriching and happy life. Remember when we talked about E + R = O? We all have the ability to *choose our response* in any given moment. We can *choose* our words from the dramatic group, or we can choose words from the empowering group. One group of words will cause us to feel disempowered, flat, frustrated and overwhelmed; the other will make us feel like we have an obstacle in front of us, but not so big that we cannot go over, around, or through it. In many ways our emotions — generated by the words we use and the images that we focus on — will either take us forward or backward. I never enjoy backtracking or walking over the same ground I have covered in the past, so I choose that which takes me forward, and I hope you do too.

4. The language we use has the ability to directly affect not only our emotional state but also our internal physiology. The downward slope for the body might look something like this (which is a continuation from our E + R = O lesson):

    a. Something happens (Event).

    b. You choose to focus on the negative (Response).

c. You use negative words to describe the event and yourself, such as disaster, ruin, tragedy, failure, catastrophe, loser, idiot, stupid, etc.

d. You start to experience negative emotions, which leads to feeling like crap. You slip into a fight or flight response.

e. Your shoulders start to droop and your head comes down, restricting your chest cavity, so your breathing becomes more shallow, meaning less oxygen reaches your lungs and body, your stomach constricts, adversely affecting digestion, your body starts to produce more acid, and as your head and vision are focused downwards, a downward emotional spiral is exacerbated.

When your body goes into survival and protection mode (the fight or flight response) it reduces the functioning of the neocortex, the most developed part of our brain and the area that enables us to be creative, solve problems and be resourceful. This is the area of the brain that we definitely want to tap into, but it shuts down in a negative emotional spiral. In a sense, negative emotional spirals make us dumber. Not exactly the best path to happiness and success.

Just writing about that miserable downward spiral of negativity made me feel crappy, and I actually got up and jumped around the room, which brings up an effective strategy for snapping out of such a spiral — get up and jump around. Go for a jog or step outside for a few moments: Change your physiology and your focus changes — and your emotions will change with it.

Anthony Robbins is famous for creating (among other things) what he calls 'The Triad', that is, changing your emotional state in a heartbeat, by changing your physiology, focus and LANGUAGE. Applying just one of these can change your emotional state; all three will guarantee you go to a whole new place. Robbins also says that 'motion creates emotion'. I reinterpret that slightly and say that 'motion changes emotion'. Physical activity actually stimulates the release of different feel-good chemicals in your body, such as serotonin and dopamine. Therefore the next time you find yourself in a wee funk, get up and start shaking that booty. Put on your best tunes and move that body, and a positive emotional state will come along with you for the ride.

Another pioneer making a huge positive impact around the world on the power of words is Dr Darren Weissman, author of *The Power of Infinite Love and Gratitude* and creator of the very powerful LifeLine Technique™. Initially trained as a chiropractor, Dr Weissman gained further certification in Applied Kinesiology (AK), Total Body Modification (TBM), Neuro Emotional Technique (NET), Neuro Linguistic Programming (NLP), Neuro Modulation Technique (NMT), Chinese energetic medicine, natural healing, and many other forms of energy healing.

In conducting muscle testing (such as the kinaesthetic exercise we did in Chapter 9 on Integrity) Dr Weissman found, quite by chance, that signing (in sign language) the word *love* over the arm and projecting the thought or intention of love at the person, strengthened the arm during the test. Just the thought or focus on the word love affects the energetic field of another person (if you want to understand the science behind this, feel free to delve into some Quantum Physics research!). Dr Weissman went on to realize and prove that if he said the words 'Infinite Love and Gratitude' while projecting that intention to a patient he was working with, their muscle strength increased.

There is so much more that I could say about Dr Weissman's work and findings, and the miraculous results he is getting with a multitude of patients' physical and psychological issues; but the point I want to make is that the words we use and the intention that we hold when we say them is more powerful than we can possibly imagine. Neuroscience, epigenetics, cellular biology and quantum physics are starting to catch up to understanding the kind of results people like Dr Weissman are seeing, and confirming that the words and language we use internally and externally heavily impacts our results in life and maintaining a high default level of happiness. Be conscious and careful of the words that you use both externally and most importantly internally if you want to lead a happy and abundant life.

And on that note, the old saying, 'Sticks and stones may break my bones, but names will never hurt me' is WRONG! Names and words definitely matter.

Summary

1. Whether or not you consciously choose them, the words you use create negative, neutral or positive emotional responses, internally and externally of you. Consciously choose words that empower and support you, and you will make better choices. Better choices lead to better results in life. When I stopped choosing negative words and started using more positive ones, my whole life changed for the better. I realized that it wasn't that life was punishing me, but that the poor thoughts and words I was choosing had a much heavier impact than I had thought possible.

2. The words you use matter. Even if they are not spoken, the words you say to yourself have an enormous impact on your self-image and self-worth. Speaking to yourself with love will help others speak to you with love as well.

3. Leave drama for television. *Choosing* to describe your life and everything that happens in it using highly charged *emotive language* invites drama into your life. Get your love, attention and affection through healthy relationships and authentic connections, rather than by creating a personal disaster zone that people want to look at as they drive by on their way to something more enjoyable. Your drama might provide mild interest or entertainment at best, but it is unlikely to be a place where people wish to spend a lot of time.

4. Words can affect you at a physical level. They can make you stronger or weaker. Do you want to try another exercise to prove it? And if you are still riding public transport or on a plane, here is another chance to connect with your new friend. (When you empower them with this technique they are going to be so impressed with you, that date is assured!) Using the same technique as before (see the kinaesthetic exercise in Chapter 9), ask

your friend to name something they believe they are not good at, then follow these steps:

a. Test their arm at full strength, just to get the measure of their strength — this is called calibrating the arm.

b. Ask them to declare 'I CANNOT do … (the thing they said they were not good at)' and test their muscle strength.

c. Ask them to then declare 'I CAN do … (the thing they said they were not good at)' and test their muscle strength. Make sure they say 'CAN' in a positive tone of voice, the same way they would declare something they are certain of achieving, such as, 'I CAN walk for 5 minutes without stopping'.

d. In the vast majority of cases the person will have more strength when they say the words 'I CAN', than when they say 'I CANNOT'. The difference is in a mere three letters! If dropping three letters can improve your strength, what can a whole day's worth of positive, affirming dialogue do for your strength, energy and life force? You would be a force to be reckoned with!

Happiness Strategies

1. Pay extremely close attention to the words you use for the next 7 days. Listen to the language that people are using around you. Is it positive or negative? Empowering or disempowering? If it is negative or disempowering, excuse yourself, or just turn around and run in the opposite direction as fast as you can!

2. Pay attention over the next 7 days to the words you use internally. Are you being kind to yourself or a total bitch? If you are being a bitch, then demand that security throw him or her out of the corridors of your mind by choosing positive language internally.

3. Do the I CAN / I CANNOT exercise within the next 24 hours. Be brave and change that person's life beside you for the better as you teach them how they can better choose their language, and allow them to help you in the same way.

4. Read Dr Darren Weissman's book, *The Power of Infinite Love and Gratitude* to more fully understand the power of our words on our bodies and minds. Also check out the movie, *What the Bleep Do We Know?*, or read Louise Hay's book, *You Can Heal Your Life*, both of which highlight the impact of the language we use on our body, mind and happiness in life.

CHAPTER 18:

Ease up on the *shoul*ding and *must*abating

Surrender your demand to be perfect.
Albert Ellis, American psychologist

No, that is not a misspelling, and don't worry, *The Guidebook to Happiness* is not about to take a completely different path. To clear up mustabating right from the start, Albert Ellis, the founder of Rational Emotive Behavior Therapy (REBT), and considered to be one of the most influential psychotherapists of all time, is credited with coining the term.

In the same category of *must*abating are also the terms SHOULD, OUGHT TO, MUST, GOT TO, HAVE TO, etc. I put all of these words into a box labelled 'Speaking in Absolutes'. Speaking in absolutes is when you make a statement about a person, place, event or object as though it is 100% true, when the reality is that you are not 100% certain, thus the statement is not 100% true. It leaves you believing strongly in an untrue statement. A state that sounds a little uncomfortable to me.

Don Miguel Ruiz, a traditional Mexican shamanic teacher and healer, in his book, *The Four Agreements*, suggests four great philosophies for life. One of them is, 'Don't make assumptions'. Not making assumptions is a a key to a deeper level of happiness — and fewer arguments. If we are not 100% sure of a statement, in 100% of cases, then that statement is in fact an assumption. And as I mentioned earlier, Byron Katie, author of *Loving What Is*, says that when she argues with reality, she loses, but only 100% of the time.

While I am going to focus on the effects of using the word 'SHOULD', consider any of the terms contained in my 'Speaking in Absolutes' box interchangeable with it. (In my personal experience, 'should' is the word most commonly used of the lot, and most often leads to emotional angst and pain. Not fun.)

This is how *should*ing works: I say X *should* lead to Y (based on an assumption). If X does lead to Y, I am happy. If X does not lead to Y, I am unhappy. That is the easy part. Now we are going to dig a bit deeper. If Y is the end result, then the likelihood of X leading to Y is hugely affected by how much control I have over the process. If I have absolute control, I can strongly influence the result. If I have no control over the process (if the control rests with someone or something else), then I have very little influence over the results.

Let me use a real life example to illustrate this. I submit my Visa Application to the Myanmar Embassy while I am staying in Indonesia and make the statement, based on my observations, that my application *should* get approved within a week and it *should* cost $150 to process. Cue reality! The *reality* is that the Embassy rejects my Visa Application and keeps my $150 to cover administration fees. If you guessed that I now feel 'pissed off' you would be correct. The gap between what I thought *should* happen and what actually did happen left me wide open to disappointment. An effective happiness strategy is to continually stick to the facts and then develop a *solution* based on those facts.

How about this example? You have an important work presentation that you are keen to deliver in the morning. You believe it *should* take you 30 minutes to get to work, but you get caught in a traffic jam and it takes you 90 minutes, making you late for the presentation. How do you feel? There is a gap between your expectation and the reality of the situation. The size of this gap is likely to determine your level of annoyance and frustration.

But unfortunately the scenario above does not stop there. Once you get annoyed or frustrated at the traffic you start to fume. You yell at the cars in front of you, bang your hands on the steering wheel, and get so irritated that you raise your middle finger to a 70-year-old struggling to negotiate the traffic. Then because you have been reading a book on anger management you decide that you *should not* be getting angry. This makes you feel even worse and before you know it, you are in a downward spiral that feeds itself. Albert Ellis suggests that a lot of therapy cases originate from people's beliefs about what they *should* or s*hould not* be feeling. Someone feels anger for whatever reason and then starts to feel even worse because they start thinking I should not be feeling this way (when the reality is they are). But I shouldn't! But you are. I know, but I shouldn't! But you are ...

The other problem with speaking in absolutes is that when we say, 'It *should* be so', we are limiting our happiness to just one possibility, when the reality is that there are many different possibilities and ways of doing things in life. If we stop speaking in absolutes it can mean the difference between walking in a narrow alley of anxiety and moving freely across an open field of possibility. Compare the phrases in the two columns below. Which would make you feel restricted and which more relaxed?

Alley of anxiety	Field of possibility
We MUST do it this way	We could do it this way or that way
She OUGHT TO arrive in 10 minutes	She will get here when she gets here
He SHOULD apologize	It would be nice if he apologized
I HAVE TO be number 1	I will work hard to become number 1
You SHOULD wear your jacket	Wear your jacket if you want

Did you notice that the phrases in the Alley of anxiety column are assumptions? And that in the Field of possibility column, there is not just one option? The significance is huge. If you choose to speak in a way that is represented by the field of possibility, you allow yourself the option of being happy regardless of final outcomes. You become more relaxed because you are not fighting with reality. In fact you are partnering with reality, in effect saying, 'I would really like things to work out my way, but I will still be ok if reality turns out differently.'

When we make an absolute statement such as, 'Those people MUST be the cause of the bad service we're getting' we generally want to protect our statement, so we don't look uninformed, or like an ass. What happens if someone counters you and says, 'Maybe those people are not to blame'? Because we made an assumption, we now feel we have to strongly defend our statement so we don't look stupid for making it in the first place. Can you see how speaking in absolutes and making assumptions might very well be a cause of pointless arguments, wasted energy and less happy times?

What do you think my chances are of winning a court case if I am defending a statement that is not a fact, nor based on reality? I will either lose or have to expend a lot of energy defending myself. In an equation:

Wasted energy = wasted life force = less happiness.

Here is the remedy for not looking like an idiot or needing to defend yourself:

1. Get out of the habit of making assumptions (by becoming more conscious of the words you use) and definitely don't bet your house on something that may not be 100% true.

2. Preface any assumptions by saying, 'In my opinion', 'My observation is', 'In my experience', 'My assumption is', 'I like to think that', 'Perhaps it is', 'Maybe', etc.

3. Be ok with being wrong.

If you want to have more peace, calm and happiness in your life as you merrily stroll across that field of possibility, either refrain from making assumptions in the first place or make it clear that the statement you are about to make is your best guess, and may not be 100% correct.

Summary

1. It is in your best interest not to talk in absolutes. Reduce the amount of *should*ing and *must*abating that you do each day. It will greatly reduce your stress levels.

2. Assuming that something *should* be a particular way instead of accepting the way it really is will cause you stress, discomfort, anger or frustration.

3. It is much easier to take action and come up with solutions when you are dealing with facts. They are more solid, whereas assumptions are like slippery eels. (Not that I have anything against eels.)

4. A lot of people cause themselves excessive and unnecessary emotional stress when they believe they *should not* be feeling a certain way. Accept how you feel in any given situation and use it as an opportunity to find a solution from that incredible mind of yours.

5. Protecting assumptions is neither a fun nor valuable use of your time and energy. Stick to protecting facts and you will be a whole lot happier.

Happiness Strategies

1. Place yourself on a *should* diet for the next 7 days. No *shoulds* allowed!

2. Pay particular attention to when you are tempted to use *should* and correct yourself by focusing on the reality of the situation. Ask yourself, *why* should it be so? This turns your beautiful conscious mind onto action mode and is likely to open the door to many other possibilities, which you may have previously overlooked.

3. The next time you get annoyed, frustrated, or angry, pay attention to where your thinking takes you. Were you about to dive into *should*ing? Notice it. Catch yourself out. Work on a solution based on the reality to take yourself out of it.

CHAPTER 19:

'For me to find true fulfilment in life ...'

A promise is a cloud; fulfilment is rain.
Proverb

How would you finish that sentence 'For me to find true fulfilment in life...'? What do you think are the necessary ingredients for feeling a sense of deep fulfilment and contentment in life? Imagine experiencing the feelings derived from knowing, believing that *you* really matter and what you are *doing* really matters and what you are *achieving* really matters. Wouldn't that be wonderful to experience on a consistent basis? Imagine looking back over the past week, month and year and having a deep sense of fulfilment wash over you. Imagine you feel no anxiety about where you are right now and where you are heading in your life. How about I share a couple of the main ingredients, as determined by one of the greatest modern thought-leaders, who has been spreading his message for over 30 years.

Anthony Robbins has worked with millions of people over the years and is tuned in to what drives human behavior at a psychological level. He has studied so many other people before him who contemplated that same question, from the early Greek philosophers, the 20th century psychologists, and the greats such as Abraham Maslow, who came up with the 'hierarchy of human needs'. In this chapter, I draw on Robbins' highlighting of what he believed to be our basic human needs.

Robbins suggests we need two essential elements to experience fulfilment in our lives. The first one is a need for 'growth'. We need to feel we are growing in life to feel fulfilled. The second is our deep human need for 'contribution'. Just let those two settle in: Growth and contribution, growth and contribution. Do you agree as you think about those two ingredients in relation to your own life? Do you feel a deep sense of fulfilment when you are growing? Do you feel a sense of fulfilment wash over you when you are contributing beyond yourself? Having worked with a lot of people over the years, I have learned that if either of those elements doesn't exist in someone's life they are unlikely to be truly happy.

Growth

Let's first explore the basic human need for growth. When we talk about a 'need' we are talking about something almost tangible that is well below the conscious or visible surface and wants to see the light of day. Some of our basic human needs lie so deeply below the surface of our conscious awareness that sometimes we cannot put our finger on exactly what is making us feel dissatisfied. It is important to our happiness to recognize and support our basic needs, because if they remain unsatisfied, it is hard for us to feel fully alive.

Science ascertains that the universe is constantly expanding and continuing to grow into infinity. And if a universe expanding into infinity doesn't make your head spin enough, as I said before Albert Einstein's well-known equation, $E=mc^2$, suggests that everything in the universe is, at the quantum level, made up of energy vibrating at different levels of frequencies. My contention is therefore that if the universe is expanding, and we are made of the same stuff as the universe, then we have a basic internal need to be expanding, growing, as well. If we aren't growing or expanding our consciousness, we are fighting against the deep inherent need to do so. I truly believe that at every level of our being we feel deeply compelled to grow physically, emotionally, mentally, and spiritually.

That is why the high-jumper wants to jump higher, the runner wants to run faster, the yogi wants to expand their consciousness more, the billionaire wants to make even more money, and why you and I would like to experience happiness, contentment, joy, knowledge, peace and fulfilment to a fuller extent and on a more consistent basis.

Using nature as a guide, what happens to a plant that is not growing? A plant that is not growing is dying. The same applies to you, albeit not as dramatically. If you do not feel that you are growing, be it physically, emotionally, mentally, or spiritually, then there is a good chance you may feel that something is missing in your life. It is like a pool of water that stays still for too long — it becomes stagnant. When water is constantly moving, it remains fresh, clean and healthy.

Let's look at a person who is going through life playing a very safe game. Doing the same thing they have always done. Working in the same job they have always had. Going to the same club. Eating the same meals. Living a safe and secure life because they have a fear of the unknown or lack trust in life, or hold any number of beliefs that root them to the spot. Chances are that though the person may be safe and secure, they are also likely to be deeply unfulfilled. There is a price to pay for not growing — spending time walking an unhappy and unfulfilled path.

Why is it important for you to continually challenge your body so the muscles and your physical prowess can improve? And why is it so important to challenge yourself emotionally by expressing more of your uniqueness, pushing through your resistance and letting the world see more of who and what you are? Why is it important to keep challenging your mind to think more deeply and fully? Why is it important to explore and understand your spirituality at a deeper level? In all of these cases, if you stop moving forward, you start moving backward. If you stop challenging your muscles they start breaking down; if you don't expand your emotional bandwidth you become overly sensitive to many daily stressors; if you stop challenging your mind your mental faculties deteriorate; and if you don't expand or explore your spirituality you feel more disconnected.

So how do we grow? To make our muscles grow, we work against a resistance, or weight. If there is no resistance, there is a likelihood of atrophy, where muscles lose size and strength. If the weight is too low, there is little resistance and therefore little or no growth. In the gym, the greater the resistance, the greater the muscle growth.

The same principle also applies to our mind. If we don't challenge our mind then it will not only fail to grow and expand, but will atrophy as well. Regularly practicing mental activities, such as puzzles and crosswords, helps reduce the likelihood of the onset of dementia in later life. Gone is the antiquated idea that our mind and our intelligence level is set from birth. Neuroscience has proven that new neurons are being created in the brain throughout our entire lives and that the mind has neuroplasticity, meaning it can actually grow and change. You have the ability to expand your intelligence by the books you read, the company you keep, the programs you listen to, and the thinking you actively perform.

Contribution

'It is one of the beautiful compensations of this life that no man can sincerely try to help another without helping himself.'
Ralph Waldo Emerson

You know I love to start a topic with a question. Do you know of anyone that has a lot of money but is absolutely miserable? I am sure that you, like I, have met people who fall into this category. On the other hand, do you know of anyone that was in that situation but they ended up experiencing deep satisfaction upon realizing the joy of giving, just like a real-life Scrooge?

I am certain, if you are reading this book, that you are the type of person that has contributed to someone beyond yourself at some point in your life. Recall the instance. Pause for 30 seconds to remember the way you felt ...

… you still have 15 seconds …

I am hypothesizing that it made you feel pretty good, and that you feel the benefits of having contributed not only at the time of giving but also at any time you recall the experience. We are talking about some powerful stuff here. Research suggests that when we give to others, the person receiving feels great due to a release of feel-good hormones such as serotonin and oxytocin; plus the person doing the giving feels great — but a person who observes the exchange between giver and receiver also experiences a release of the same feel-good hormones. That is a wellness slam-dunk if I ever heard one.

At a psychological level, when we give to someone else, we are reaffirming for ourselves that we have plenty to give. It gives us an elevated feeling of well-being and self-worth. It is not a feeling of superiority, but we feel successful because we have more than we need for ourselves. A lot of successful businesspeople cite tithing, that is, giving a percentage of their profit to charity, as one of the contributions (pun not intended) to their success. They believe that their business improved and increased when they consistently gave. At a practical level a lot of companies have enhanced their brand, image and profits as a result of being more socially responsible and actively contributing to social causes.

Chapter 3 discussed cause and effect and how for every action there is an equal and opposite reaction. When you give to another, you are starting a positive chain of events that could continue around the world until it comes back to you in a different form. In the movie *Pay It Forward*, a ripple effect starts from a small boy's three random acts of kindness and ends up touching thousands of people's lives. When you help one person you also positively affect their family, friends and everyone else they cross paths with in their lives moving forward. How cool is that?

To build happiness, it is important to contribute consistently. Psychologically, it builds on the feeling that you are doing well in life, and you have enough to help out others. You do not have to give thousands of dollars, or indeed, contributing needn't involve money at all. You can donate your time to a cause or an organization you believe in; for example, joining your local food co-operative or volunteering at the city's soup kitchen. The amount is less important than the sincerity of the contribution and the positive intention you hold when helping others less fortunate.

I also believe there is a difference between giving to someone in our circle of closest friends and family, and someone that is completely unknown to us. Giving to our nearest and dearest unconditionally is a beautiful thing, but when we give to someone that is external to our everyday life it is easier to give without any strings attached (whether intentional or unintentional), and strengthens our connection with the wider world. The benefit of our connecting with and helping a person or people with a different lifestyle, culture, religious belief, or physical appearance is so beneficial; it goes a long way towards dissolving the separation created by country borders and increasing a sense of oneness between humanity. It enhances our spiritual growth and reminds us that we are all part of the same human family, and that is a good thing for everyone.

Summary

1. In his study of the great minds before him, Anthony Robbins came up with a pretty good model when he isolated Growth and Contribution as two basic human needs for fulfilment in life.

2. If you are not growing in life, physically, mentally, emotionally and spiritually, by constantly challenging where you are right now, you're likely, at some level, to feel unfulfilled and unhappy with yourself and your life.

3. Your mind and body both need resistance to grow. Engaging in physical and mental challenges will ensure that neither atrophies. You are also growing new brain cells all the time. Know that you have an incredible

amount of untapped potential that will ensure that you could grow every day for 20 years and still have the capacity to grow even more. There is no limitation on what you can do or achieve if you fully apply your mental and physical gifts.

4. Contributing beyond yourself makes you feel great at the time and at any time you remember the event in the future. It also makes the person receiving it, and anyone that observes your act of compassion and contribution, feel great.

5. Make contribution a consistent part of your life. It will give you a psychological edge, a feeling that you have enough to give to others. It will increase your own self-worth and self-image, which will positively affect your own life.

6. When contributing, challenge yourself to reach out to someone that you don't know; someone who is from a completely different culture or demographic. This connection across physical and cultural borders will give you a heightened sense of oneness and a deeper perspective of the challenges that people experience in different parts of the world or different parts of your community.

7. Ensure there are no strings attached to your contributions — give because you want to and because you care. Don't expect anything in return beyond your own feelings of self-worth; otherwise you diminish the positive benefits for yourself and the recipient of your contribution.

Happiness Strategies

1. Expand your mind and body by learning something new in the next 90 days. Perhaps you can learn a new physical skill, or take a short course on a topic that will enhance your business or personal life. You might even like to take on the WorldsBIGGESTGym™ *30-Day Happiness Challenge*.

2. Contribute beyond yourself in the next 7 days. Remember:

    a. Contributing doesn't just mean giving money. Being there to listen to someone's story about the challenges or hardships they have faced in life makes a massive impact. Treating another person with compassion, respect and as an equal can be worth much more than just money.

    b. Never think that you don't have anything to offer. Offer what you can, when you can. It is the act of contributing and your sincerity that count.

3. Include an element of contribution in your life on an on-going basis. It might be to a person, group, or cause, or for people, animals, or the environment. Tap into the power of giving on your way to a life of deep fulfilment and happiness.

CHAPTER 20:

Doing the Sherlock Holmes

Effective people are not problem-minded; they're opportunity-minded.
Steven Covey, American author, educator and keynote speaker

I just love this law and have a sneaking suspicion that you will too. The message is essentially this: Life is *all good* if you perfect the art of doing the Sherlock Holmes. We will get to Holmes shortly, but for now let's look at why life is 'all good'.

Have you ever taken the time to really notice how everything has a corresponding opposite? Not most things, but everything. Here are just a few:

- Up and down.
- Inside and outside.
- Top and bottom.
- Back and front.
- Matter and anti-matter.
- Forwards and backwards.
- Cold and hot.

If it is 3 paces from my chair to the door, then it is 3 paces from the door to my chair. If it is 10 feet from the ceiling to the floor, then it is 10 feet from the floor to the ceiling. Nothing can exist without its corresponding equal and opposite — just like a coin cannot have only one side, an event cannot be all 'bad' — which means there is an equal and opposite amount of good in every situation.

Buddhist teachings say that everything is neutral and it is only the meaning we give to something that decides whether it is good or bad. This relates back to E + R = O discussed in Chapter 13. It is the response we choose, or the belief we activate, that determines what the outcome of any given event will be.

Knowing that it is there, we need to look for the good, not so much with our eyes as with our minds. Our incredibly powerful mind has the ability, when actively engaged, to recognize that there are always many other perspectives to any situation, and can find the good that inevitably exists.

It is the way in which we interpret what our eyes see that matters. Our vision works like this: the sun shines on the planet illuminating everything by its light reflecting off the surface. When we open our eyes, the reflected light comes in through our cornea (then pupil, lens and retina), travels along a series of optic nerves, and ends up in a certain part of our brain. The signal (as opposed to a 'picture') is then interpreted by the mind, based on a combination of what we believe we ought to see and what we are looking for. It is our beliefs about what we expect to see that actually influence what we see within the picture we are looking at. That is why two people can look at the same thing and see something completely different; for example, witnesses to the same crime can give vastly different accounts of it. In most cases we see what we want to see, based on what we believe we ought to see.

The great thing about looking for the good in every situation is that it does not require a cash deposit, a pint of blood, a lifetime commitment to a time-share apartment in the middle of Boringsville, or years of sitting like a pretzel in the lotus position. It simply requires you to ask yourself, 'What is good or great about this event?' or 'What *could* be good or great about this event?'

Can you see how the question completely channels your laser-like focus? It also encourages you to transform your mind-set to be far more empowering. You say to yourself, 'there is something good here because I know that nothing bad can exist without a corresponding equal and opposite good, so I will keep looking until I find it'.

Let's put this into a real-life scenario: You are driving home from work and your car breaks down. According to your Buddhist friends, the event is neutral until you assign it meaning. Label the event a positive learning experience using your super-powerful tool — by asking, 'What is good or great about my car breaking down?'

1. It could be worse — I could have been in an accident. Taking a fresh perspective I feel relief and gratitude for being safe.

2. I'll avoid having to go to my partner's boss's dinner party, which I didn't want to attend.

3. While I wait for assistance, I have time to listen to some great music and catch up on a motivational program, which makes me feel better.

4. The tow truck company and mechanic will be appreciative of the business I will give them.

5. I walk the last 3 km (1.9 miles) home, which is great exercise and leaves me feeling fresh and renewed.

And the list goes on …

This is not about looking at the world through rose-colored glasses and blithely assuming that everything is great. It is about focusing on the good, so that you feel positive emotions in your body. We all know that shitty things happen and shitty people exist in the world — but fixating on them does not make them go away. Fixating on the bad not only makes you miserable, but disempowers you as well. It drains you of energy, and kills creativity and progression. Alternatively, creating a positive mental attitude and looking for the good that exists in every situation empowers you, energizes you, improves your immune system and helps you become solution-oriented. It helps you feel comforted, grateful and inspired. The good is always there, you just have to find it with your new questioning tool.

Looking for the positive in every experience is what I call 'Doing the Sherlock Holmes'. You might need to prod and poke, change angles, uncover things, dig deeper, and step back and re-evaluate to find the good in certain situations. But like Sherlock Holmes, the more you practise asking 'what is great about this?' the better you will become at finding the answers. And the better you become at finding those answers, the more positive emotions you will experience, and the happier you will feel. You will feel that life is for you and not against you, and that everything that happens in life is happening to help you grow and experience life more fully.

Summary

1. Everything has a corresponding opposite. Nothing is all bad.

2. According to Buddhist teachings, all events are neutral until we apply a meaning to them. *We get to choose* the way we label each event.

3. We generally see what we expect to see. If we believe that there is an equal amount of good within a situation, then we will see that good.

4. Your best tool in any situation that appears to be 'bad' is to ask one of those powerful questions, 'What is good or great about this situation?', or 'What could be good or great about this situation?'

Happiness Strategies

1. Identify a 'negative' emotional event.

2. Do the Sherlock Holmes and search hard to find the good in it.

3. Write down the good that you took from the event so you start to view the event as a positive learning experience. This act of changing

the picture you have in your mind is called 'reframing' and is a very powerful NLP tool. The better you get at reframing, the greater the levels of happiness you will experience on a daily basis.

4. Be willing to let go of any negative emotion you had attached to the event (which is easier with all the positive lessons you took from it).

5. Express gratitude for the valuable lessons and experience the event brought you. It is through knowledge and experience that our wisdom and mind grow.

CHAPTER 21:

There is no such thing as failure, only feedback

I have not failed. I've just found 10,000 ways that won't work.
Thomas Edison, American inventor and businessman

The more I study the most successful people on the planet, the longer the list of setbacks and failures I come across. Failure seems synonymous with success. The more people fail, the more they seem to achieve. Consider these examples. Donald Trump's first major business failure put him an astonishing $900 million in the red. Henry Ford's first business went bust, as did Walt Disney's. The same can be said of the early business ventures of the people behind Hershey's chocolate, and Heinz baked beans. And during Abraham Lincoln's stint as a shop owner, he dove into serious debt. It took him years to pay it off, even after he sold his horse and some surveying gear. It seems to me that past 'failures' have no negative impact on what you can achieve in the future. These people learned the art of failure — how to reframe their experiences to work in their favor.

A word on what I mean by 'success': in psychology there is a direct correlation between happiness and success. I take 'success' to be less about financial worth and more about achieving one's goals. Even the idea of failure has such a profound affect on someone's default level of happiness (in a negative direction). So one of the keys to happiness is not only to be ok with the word 'failure', but also to see it as a necessary step on the path to success, fulfilment and abundant happiness in life. This is also the last chapter because when you apply the lessons and strategies that you have learned in *The Guidebook to Happiness*, you are likely to have some setbacks. In the past you would have called them 'failures' and given yourself a hard time, or worse, given up. By the end of this chapter you will realize that the 'failures' are actually the 'feedback' you really need in order to grow and reach your full potential and increase your default level of happiness.

In an interview with Robin Sharma (from January 2012), Darren Hardy, publisher of SUCCESS Magazine and a highly successful businessman, told of how his mother left not long after he was born. His father, a no-nonsense, straight-shooting, results-focused man, raised him on his own. When Darren was asked how he came to be so successful and what beliefs he had established to elevate him to his position, he recalled a story from his childhood. Around the age of 8, Darren returned home from a full day of skiing on his own and proudly declared to his father that he had not fallen down all day. His father's response was 'well then you didn't get any better'. Darren's father told him that if you are not falling over, then you are not pushing yourself enough and therefore you will not improve. He encouraged him to fall over, because then he would know that Darren was challenging himself and, as a result, improving. Talk about setting up an 8-year-old for success.

Imagine going through your life not only being *unafraid* of failure but also believing that if you were not failing every now and again, then you were not pushing yourself hard enough. What an incredible belief to hold onto and what an incredible way to become fearless. Tal Ben-Shahar, author of *The Pursuit of Perfect*, says:

> 'One of the wishes that I always have for my students is that they should fail more often (although they are understandably not thrilled to hear me tell them so). If they fail frequently, it means that they try frequently, that they put themselves on the line and challenge themselves. It is only from the experience of challenging ourselves that we learn and grow, and we often develop and mature much more

from our failures than from our successes. Moreover, when we put ourselves on the line, when we fall down and get up again, we become stronger and more resilient.'

Here are some more examples of the failures or setbacks of high achievers:

- The *Chicken Soup* for the Soul book series by Mark Viktor Hanson and Jack Canfield was rejected over 100 times. Since its eventual publication, it has become a worldwide phenomenon and boasts over 200 titles in the series, has sold over 100 million copies, and has been translated into more than 50 different languages.

- Seven years after graduating from the University of Exeter in England, this author was coming out of a failed marriage, jobless and had a dependant child. In a 2008 TED Talk entitled 'The fringe benefits of failure' she made the now famous quote, 'And so rock bottom became a solid foundation on which I rebuilt my life.' The author is J K Rowling and her *Harry Potter* series has become the best-selling book series in history according to the Guinness World Records.

- This author received 30 rejections and eventually threw the manuscript in the rubbish. But fortunately for him, his supportive wife fished it out and encouraged him to resubmit it. The book was *Carrie* and the author was Stephen King.

- Michael Jordan, one of the most famous basketballers of all time, was cut from his high school basketball team. Fortunately, he had a great mother on Team Jordan who told him that he 'will just have to work harder'. And that is exactly what he did. He worked hard to reach a level over and above any other player to become a truly great athlete.

- In 1923, Winston Churchill had already experienced some stunning defeats and was, for the first time in 22 years, out of parliament. He mounted a comeback and was defeated twice more and by the 1930s his political career seemed to be over. But he still retained a burning desire — to be the Prime Minister of England. By persistence and tenacity he not only made his way back into parliament, but eventually went on to achieve his goal of becoming Prime Minister and was an instrumental figure in the outcome of the Second World War. He is quoted as saying, 'Success is the ability to go from failure to failure without losing your enthusiasm.'

People who have bounced back from failure to succeed are too numerous to list, and would of course include not only famous names, but also every person ever born that was able to overcome the challenge of learning to walk; every person with a handicap that has overcome it to lead a meaningful and rewarding life; and you and I. We have all attempted things that at first we truly sucked at (and have the scars to prove it) but pushed on to become good or great at. Look back at some of your successes — big or small — and remember your first day. Chances are that you faced and overcame at least one setback, if not a good deal more.

Failure is part of the process of life and a key ingredient to success, and ultimately happiness. In the early days of my business, I came up with what I thought was an outstanding marketing campaign that would reach thousands of people and elevate the profile of the business enormously. When I ran the campaign it tanked; failed miserably. Rather than reach thousands of people as I had eagerly expected, I reached the grand total of 11! In the past, this would have crushed me, but by that time I knew it was just a part of the learning process. I asked myself, 'How can I turn this around and make something great come from it?' This process resulted in a great project, involving great people, and a great final product.

When he was first starting out John Gray, author of the hugely successful book *Men are from Mars, Women are from Venus,* had organized a decent-sized seminar on meditation in a college hall. He had posted up fliers all over the college campuses and throughout town in preparation and awaited the crowd. What he said about it later sums up what happened on the night, 'Do you want to know what is much worse than no one turning up to your seminar? One person turning up!' To his credit, he held the seminar for that one person and used the opportunity to practise his presentation skills.

This leads me to discuss what I believe to be one of the most important attitudes to success in any endeavor, be it personal or professional — PERSISTENCE. It is persistence that will cause someone to find the way or the answer. It is persistence that makes someone try another way, when all the other ways have led to nothing. It is persistence that will keep someone looking for that opening in the profession they most want to be in. It is persistence that will make a business eventually succeed when all the other businesses around it are giving up. It is persistence that gets that major publishing deal when 30 other publishers have turned you down. It is persistence that will take you to the end of that half-marathon that you signed up for on a drunken whim a couple of weeks prior (it hurt like hell, but I did it!). Persistence is the best attitude to adopt for success. It is also essential on the path to happiness. As with any other worthy goal, experiencing a higher default level of happiness in your life will require you to persistently practise the lessons you have been taught in *The Guidebook to Happiness.*

Also, it's important not to listen too much to others. Especially don't pay much attention to people that are not qualified to give you advice (which unfortunately is a lot of people). Seek out and listen to someone that has grown from an apparent failure to achieve success; understand what they did and pay particular attention to the mind-set that they created or maintained. Success and happiness are so dependent on understanding *who you need to become* in order to experience the results that you want. So take a step back from your 'failure' and ask yourself did you show up as the right person? Were you courageous enough? Were you persistent enough? Were you completely focused on the result you wanted? Is there something in you that needs to be addressed? The great thing about finding something within you that needs to be expressed more fully, is that it does not require someone or something else external to you. Find the courage, persistence and focus within yourself, and then bring them more fully to the light of day. There is a great NLP saying, 'All you need is within you now.'

Failure is a necessary part of the journey to success and happiness. The name of one of the books by John C Maxwell, an internationally recognized leadership expert, speaker, coach, and best-selling author, is *Failing Forward*. How appropriate.

Summary

1. If you are not failing it might be that you are not trying hard enough. Embrace the tumbles, bumps, scrapes and bruises. A fulfilling life is made of these.

2. Failing may be the very feedback you need to succeed. Look for the messages and feedback in the failure.

3. In a lot of cases, the bigger the failure the bigger the success. I am not at this stage suggesting that you do something completely reckless, which you believe will catapult you into stardom. Let's not become (in)famous for all the wrong reasons.

4. *Persistence* is the attitude you want to wear as your success and happiness cloak.

5. Don't listen too hard to what other people say, because they might just be wrong. As an unknown source tells us, 'Those who can — do. Those who can't — criticize.'

Happiness Strategies

1. For the next 30 days, face your fears and do it anyway. You have everything to gain.

2. On a fresh page in your journal, write down an event in your life that you label as a failure or setback. Split the page into two columns, each named 'Positive lessons I learned' and 'How I can use those positive lessons to

my best advantage in the future'. Get writing. (Writing the details down helps you become less emotional and therefore able to more effectively use your mind when searching for answers to your questions.)

3. Once you reframe an event from a negative to a positive (because now the event is helping you learn and grow) you will also feel empowering emotions when you think about the event.

Conclusion

Where to start? Or rather, how to end? First of all I want to say thank you. Not just for buying this book but for giving me the reason to write this book. My head has been so full of all of this information, so now I have written it down (or more accurately, two-finger typed it!) there is space for some new stuff. As a completely random aside I was thinking about how many times my two index fingers have hit a button on my keyboard. 50,000 words x 4 letters (the average letters in the words I use from my vast vocabulary) = 200,000 times my fingers have tapped the keyboard. Wow!! The things we can achieve when we have a compelling reason. Like helping you become the best person that you can possibly be! I cannot think of a better reason. So again, thank you.

It has been a great journey for me and I hope that it has been a great journey for you as well. I hope you have applied a number of the Happiness Strategies I have suggested in each chapter and I hope you are starting to already see a shift in your focus, your language, what you pay attention to and the level of awareness that you bring to your decision making. Remember that the better the choices you make in life (now you have a deeper level of understanding) the better results you are likely to achieve. That is very exciting stuff.

Now, as you know my background is in strategic and operational planning for big organizations and projects, and one thing we always did when we delivered a big report is include an Executive Summary. This was the bit that the senior executive read, that summarized the key information in the report (so they did not have to read the full report in detail to get the key information), before they handed the report off to their minions to put into action. I also decided to include an Executive Summary for you on the key takeaways from the 21

Lessons that you have been presented with. At one point I was thinking this might encourage people to not read the full book and just get a very broad view of the Lessons offered in the book. But hey, if that is what you decide to do, and providing you learn and apply at least one thing from doing that, well I am totally ok with that. I am only interested in the result: if you have achieved a higher default level of happiness at the end of the book than you had when you started, then I am chuffed!

Therefore on the pages following this Conclusion you will find *The Guidebook to Happiness* Executive Summary made especially for you — the Senior Executive, Skipper, CEO, Captain, Grand Pooh-Bah, Kingpin, General, Big Kahuna, and Managing Director of the supremely happy business called *You Inc*.

Like a person training in the gym to build the perfectly muscled and sculpted body, the academic who studies hard to mould the perfectly creative mind, the spiritual seeker who meditates to deepen their connection with a higher power; at no point on their journey do they stop and say, 'Now I have created this perfect body/mind/spiritual connection, I can stop'. The moment we stop growing, as you have come to know, is the moment we start the backward slide. Now of course there will be backward steps. There will be side steps. There will be trips and there will be falls. But to ensure you continue to grow and evolve as the best you there will ever be, you will need to continue on the journey. Face new challenges, read the feedback, push enquiringly against new resistance, reach new heights, learn new insights, gain new knowledge, and practise new strategies.

However and wherever I can, I will help you along that journey. I may even walk side by side with you at times, as our own paths merge together. You may even be my teacher one day if we get the chance to stand face to face.

If you'd like to hear more from me, and continue learning more and keeping these new insights alive in your life, join me on my *Strategic Happiness iTunes Channel*. And of course you can check out other programs on the WorldsBIGGESTGym™ website. Learning is something you want to do for the rest of your days, otherwise all those extra brain cells that are being created are sure to go to waste. More waste is the last thing that we need. So know that I and my fellow happiness Teamsters (they like to call themselves Coaches, but I think 'Teamsters' sounds way more cool) are there to help out however we can.

Remember that you are unique. Of 7 billion people there is no one with the same index finger print as you; there is no one on this planet that is quite like you. When you dare to connect with your uniqueness and specialness and individual gifts, you really can create an amazing life; but even more importantly is that you can create an amazing life for all those other people around you. Good for you. Good for others. Good for the greater good. That is 'good to the power of three' or Good^3. Now you are totally rocking it and changing the world for the better!

So thank you again for your contribution. Thank you for giving me a reason to be writing here beside the ocean in Eastern Bali as a cool sea breeze washes over me, and the coconut trees sway in the breeze. Research by psychology professor Mihaly Csikszentmihalyi, in his excellent book *Flow,* suggests that we actually have 3 to 4 times more *flow experiences*; that is, when we are in the 'zone', when time, hunger and worries just fall away, while we are working than when we are at leisure. *Just thought I would sneak in one last lesson for you*.

Have a wonderful day, week, month, year and life. Wherever you are on this amazing, wonderful, incredible, gorgeous, magnificent, adorable, soulful and remarkable planet of ours, I wish you all the very best (from me, myself and I) and take care.

It's now time to go back to the front of the book (or flick open The Guidebook to Happiness Personal Journal). Get out that trusty pencil of yours and write down what level you are now at, after reading and applying the Lessons and Happiness Strategies you learnt in The Guidebook to Happiness. Yippeeee!!

Executive summary

We are what we repeatedly do. Excellence, then, is not an act, but a habit.
Aristotle, Ancient Greek philosopher

Responsibility

Take personal responsibility for your life, otherwise you are handing the control of your life to another, or you are standing on your own boat without your hands on the steering wheel.

Energy

All life is energy. Increasing energy, knowledge and strategies for growth in life will help us best place that additional available energy to boost our default level of happiness.

Chapter 1: It all starts in the mind

1. Visualize what you want as clearly as you possibly can. Imagine a range of colours, sounds and even textures, smells and tastes. See your goal unfolding before you exactly as you want, as if it is happening right now.

2. Get emotionally engaged with the things you really want, when you are forming the pictures in your mind. Once your emotions are fully engaged, you will be pulled along by inspiration and will love taking persistent action towards achieving your goals.

Chapter 2: Half the equation in the science of happiness

1. Start with your highest, most inspiring goal. This could also be described

as your purpose in life. The more inspired you are, the more you will be carried along. So dig deep; see if you can find something of great meaning in your life. A great purpose is one that serves you, serves others and is for the greater good of the planet (it does not matter if that is in a big or small way). Your purpose in life does not have to be earth shattering, planet changing, or saving all of humanity. Mother Teresa did not set out to alleviate the poverty of the whole world; she set as her purpose to alleviate the poverty in Calcutta and it just grew from there.

2. Once you are clear about your goals it is easier to make decisions about other opportunities that arise. If an opportunity comes to you that does not support your goals and does not warrant changing your current goals then reject the opportunity (or distraction).

Chapter 3: Down which path are your beliefs taking you?

1. The first thing we need to understand is that a belief is not a universal law, like gravity, but is something we have convinced ourselves is true. It can be changed. Our beliefs may not even be our own, but those imparted to us during the suggestive theta brainwave state when we were under 7 years of age. So do not get attached, stuck on, overly defensive of, or bet your house on a belief that you may have 'picked up along the way'.

2. Our beliefs cause us to behave in a certain way, often so repeatedly that we are unaware of it. The way we behave determines the results we get in life. If we change our beliefs for the better, we change our results for the better.

3. It is not about right or wrong beliefs. The important thing is to determine which beliefs or statements you repetitively say are EMPOWERING and which are disempowering. The aim is to tap into more of the empowering beliefs and replace disempowering beliefs with even more empowering beliefs.

Chapter 4: That Newton dude was on to something: What we give out, we get back

1. You can dispute or ignore universal laws of physics if you want, but they will still do what they have always done. For every action there is an equal and opposite reaction ... every time.

2. The more effort or energy we put into something, the greater the effect and the greater possible result. As a former engineer in the Australian Army, I can assure you that the more explosive we used, the bigger the bang, every time. It's the same with you — the more energy you put into a situation, the greater the results will be. But remember, just as an engineer blowing up a decommissioned bridge knows, *where you place the explosive* is just as important as having the right type and amount of explosive for the task. It is not just about the energy you exert, but where and how you do it. Be very conscious about where and how you direct your energy.

Chapter 5: Become a grand master through the power of Daily Rituals

1. Just as an elite athlete performs rituals to enhance their ability and attract and maintain million-dollar contracts, incorporating Daily Rituals in your life will help you become an elite performer, making a significant difference to your level of happiness and ability to achieve your goals.

2. A day in your life is like the elite athlete's match day. Just as the elite athlete practices rituals before, during and after the game to ensure the best possible performance, you too can introduce powerful and positive rituals into your own daily life, establishing lifelong positive habits that strengthen and raise your default level of happiness.

Chapter 6: Is that really what you want to know?

1. If you don't like the answers you are getting, then change the question.

2. Always ask SOLUTION-oriented questions.

Chapter 7: I could complain, or I could just enjoy myself

1. Complaining is focusing your mind's power on the things that you don't want in your life. The more energy directed at something the bigger it grows.

2. If you argue with reality you will lose, 100% of the time.

Chapter 8: Gratitude is the wonder drug of the 21st century

1. The person who is the most grateful experiences the most abundance.

2. Practicing gratitude conditions your mind to look for the good or positive benefits in any situation.

Chapter 9: The science of breath

1. Breathing is the most important thing we do, so it is in our best interest to master it. Our happiness and health depends on it.

2. We use three parts of our bodies to breathe: the diaphragm, the floating ribs and the shoulders. Practice breathing consciously with all three parts.

Chapter 10: One of the greatest virtues on Earth

1. It takes more energy, concentration and effort to tell lies. If your goal is to be lazing on the beach under coconut palms then take the easy option and start telling the truth.

2. You cannot be dishonest in one part of your life and not have it affect the other parts. The best policy is to maintain high integrity in all areas of your life.

Chapter 11: Values-based decision making

1. Clarify and understand your values and their order of priority to you so your decision making is congruent with them.

2. When you make decisions, especially the important ones, check all possible options against your values to ensure that the decisions you make align

with the values most important to you. Using the Values-Based Decision Making tool will assist you in this.

Chapter 12: The human body (and mind) works best when it moves

1. The body is designed such that the lymphatic system is dependent on movement of the skeletal muscles to perform its job of removing waste from the body, which is essential to our health. Physical activity is not an optional extra for good health and happiness; it is one of the main events.

2. Without physical activity you will never reach your *full potential*. You won't earn the money, experience the depth of relationships, have the optimum health, fully explore the world, overcome setbacks as quickly, etc., etc., as you can when you are physically active. Bottom line: Honour your body's needs and engage in regular physical activity if you wish to live a long and full life of abundant health, vitality and happiness.

Chapter 13: E + R = O

1. It is our *Response(R)* to any given *Event(E)* that determines what the final *Outcome(O)* will be.

2. We are free to decide what meaning we give to situations and then what behavior (or actions) we carry out. It is that meaning and that behavior which will have the greatest bearing on the end result.

Chapter 14: Liquid gold for the body

1. Drink plenty of water each day. Let it be the main fluid that you put into your body.

2. If you are tired or want to do your best thinking, make sure you are fully hydrated. If unsure, then drink a glass of water for good measure.

Chapter 15: Rest up or fall down

1. Taking quality mini-breaks throughout the day every 90 to 120 minutes

will improve your productivity and effectiveness.

2. Most adults (about 80%) need between 7.5 and 9 hours' sleep a day to be most effective and to avoid the trouble a tired, runaway mouth can cause.

Chapter 16: Who are your teachers?

1. Be very selective about who you spend the majority of your time with. Jim Rohn is credited with saying that 'you become the average of the five people you spend the most time with', and as Paramahansa Yogananda said, 'the environment is stronger than the willpower'. One of the reasons for this is that your environment slowly seeps into you unawares. Often, you don't put up any defences until it is too late and the change has already been made. Hence, one of the most powerful ways to consciously bring about change is to change your environment for one that is super positive and optimistic.

2. Don't take financial advice from someone that is in debt and has no money in the bank and no assets just because they regularly read the *Financial Times*. Results matter.

Chapter 17: Your words are either helping or hindering you

1. Whether or not you consciously choose them, the words you use create negative, neutral or positive emotional responses, internally and externally of you. Consciously choose words that empower and support you, and you will make better choices. Better choices lead to better results in life. When I stopped choosing negative words and started using more positive ones, my whole life changed for the better. I realized that it wasn't that life was punishing me, but that the poor thoughts and words I was choosing had a much heavier impact than I had thought possible.

2. Be mindful of the words you speak and think every day. The words you say to yourself have an enormous impact on your self-image and self-worth. Speaking to yourself with love and kindness not only increases your happiness, it will also lead you to speak to others with kindness,

thereby encouraging them to reciprocate that kindness to you.

Chapter 18: Ease up on the *should*ing and *must*abating

1. It is in your best interest not to talk in absolutes. By reducing the amount of *should*ing and *must*abating you do each day, your stress levels will be greatly reduced.

2. Assuming that something *should* be a particular way instead of accepting the way it really is, causes you stress, discomfort, anger or frustration. The word 'could' creates opening and possibility and reminds you of the choices before you, empowering you to make the best choice.

Chapter 19: 'For me to find true fulfilment in life ...'

1. Your mind and body both need resistance to grow. Engaging in physical and mental challenges will ensure that neither atrophies. Your mind is continuously growing new brain cells that are just waiting at the starting blocks for you to use them. Know that you have an incredible amount of untapped potential that will ensure that you grow, learn and develop every day for 20 years and still have the capacity to grow and expand your abilities even more. There is no limitation on what you can do or achieve if you fully apply your mental and physical gifts.

2. Contributing beyond yourself makes you feel great at the time and at any time you remember the event in the future. It also makes the person receiving it feel great and serves as a reminder to all who witness it of the importance and beauty of compassion and contribution.

Chapter 20: Doing the Sherlock Holmes

1. Everything has a corresponding opposite. Nothing is all bad. Look for the good in each situation, and you will find it.

2. According to Buddhist teachings, all events are neutral until we apply a meaning to them. We get to choose the way we label each event we

experience.

Chapter 21: There is no such thing as failure, only feedback

1. If you are not 'failing' it might be that you are not trying hard enough. Embrace the tumbles, bumps, scrapes and bruises for they are essential to a fulfilling life.

2. Failing may be the very feedback you need to succeed. Look for the messages, feedback and lessons in the failure.

Recommended reference material

Some of my greatest TEACHERS

- Albert Einstein
- Anthony Robbins
- Aristotle
- Bob Proctor
- Brendon Burchard
- Brian Johnson
- Dr Bruce Lipton
- Byron Katie
- Dr Colin T Campbell
- Dan Millman
- Darren Hardy
- Dr Darren Weissman
- Deepak Chopra
- Earl Nightingale
- Jack Canfield
- Jim Rohn
- Dr Joe Dispenza
- Dr Joel Fuhrman, MD
- Louise Hay
- Marcus Aurelius
- Rev Michael Beckworth
- Paramahansa Yogananda

- Paulo Coelho
- Robin Sharma
- Steven Covey PhD
- Tal Ben-Shahar PhD
- Wayne Dyer

You may want to look into the work of one or many of these authors and speakers to deepen your knowledge further.

WorldsBIGGESTGym™ Resources
The 30-Day Happiness Challenge

If you are ready to be truly supported, one-on-one, down the path of and to great levels of happiness, then this is for you. It is my strategic happiness masterpiece! A very strategic blend of online training, specific daily rituals, weekly coaching plus specialist work on removing limiting beliefs and how to become an ELITE Goal Setter, we believe in this very powerful transformation program so much that if you are not at a higher level of happiness (and consciousness) by the end of the Challenge you can ask for your money back.

CEOs, single mums, elite athletes, cancer patients, school teachers, small business owners, coaches, entrepreneurs, personal fitness trainers, and yoga instructors have all done the program, from wherever they are in the world. We have had clients from the Middle East, Asia, Europe, Australia, North America and Central America.

You can have me as your coach or one of my personally trained coaches.
To find out how you can continue the transformation process that you have begun and also to join me for a free live webinar make sure you click on the following link:

www.30dayhappinesschallenge.com

Become an ELITE Goal Setter Workshop

As you now know, having specific goals that contribute to your well-being, relationships and connection to others is essential for experiencing greater levels of happiness. *Future meaning* is essential for us all. We also believe that SMART Goal Setting is SO 1990s. The ELITE Goal Setter workshop goes to a whole new level by engaging the emotions — which as you know - is the cause of all motion.

This mini-workshop that is designed to teach you which steps you need to take in Goal Setting and in what specific order they must occur for optimum effect. Plus you will learn the biggest Do's and Don'ts in goal setting. The culmination of the program is a guided workshop with the end result being that you not only have clear goals, but you have also written them down in such a way that they inspire you and make it extremely clear for your subconscious mind to know exactly what you want in life. Plus you have developed a plan for achieving them. If you currently do not have any written goals this is perfect for you.

To find out how you can Become an ELITE Goal Setter make sure you go to the following link
www.elitegoalsetter.com

Free BONUS Chapters

I have come to realize over the years that it is not as fun learning a lot of amazing things if you do not share them with other people. And since we have been on this journey for a bunch of hours now, I was not quite ready to wind up my guiding responsibilities. I wanted to get in a couple of more lessons before I finished. And to tell the truth I wanted to keep the number of chapters to 21 as it has a good ring to it.

So let me offer you two additional and awesome chapters to compliment the 21 Chapters you have already read in *The Guidebook to Happiness*. They are:

1. **Happy on the inside = happy on the outside.** Studying nutrition has been a passion of mine for many years. In this chapter I share with you the best of the best that I have learned. It will educate, amaze and change your health forever.

2. **How to 'unfriend' Mr Procrastination.** If you are interested in a little productivity session, or feel you procrastinate just a little too much, then this chapter is purpose built for you.

To access the free bonus chapters (plus other very cool freebies) including regular Happiness Tips sent to you, go to this link:
www.theguidebooktohappiness.com/bonusesforbookowners

Other Books by Carl Massy
Become an ELITE Goal Setter: SMART Goal Setting is SO 1990s. Learn the new 6 steps to highly charged goal attainment (Kindle, mini-book on Amazon)

Your Beliefs are Controlling Your Life: How to turn limiting beliefs into empowering beliefs for enhanced energy and limitless potential
(eBook available at *www.theguidebooktohappiness.com*)

Corporate Training Workshops
One of my passions is conducting workshops for corporate clients. I have this belief that if you empower an individual they will make a real difference in their place of work. But if you empower a whole group from a company, then the business itself must expand as well. I call this Empowering Individuals to Enrich an Organization. If you would like me to come along and run a training workshop for your company, send an email to:
training@worldsbiggestgym.com.

Books I recommend, and some of the great resources available

I have put an * beside my most favorite books

Brain

Daniel Goleman, *The Brain and Emotional Intelligence*

David Rock, *Your Brain at Work*

Dr Joe Dispenza, *Evolve Your Brain*

Dr Joe Dispenza, *Breaking the Habit of Being Yourself* *

John Medina, PhD, *Brain Rules*

M J Gelb and K Howell, *Brain Power*

Rick Hanson, *Buddha's Brain*

General Health

Dr Dean Ornish, *Dr Dean Ornish's Program for Reversing Heart Disease*

Deepak Chopra MD, *Ageless Body, Timeless Mind*

Jim Loehr and Tony Schwartz, *The Power of Full Engagement*

John Robbins, *Healthy at 100*

Happiness

Byron Katie, *Loving What Is* *

Martin Seligman, *Authentic Happiness*

Matthieu Ricard, *Happiness*

Sonja Lyubomirsky, *The How of Happiness*

Tal Ben-Shahar, *Happier* *

Will Bowen, *A Complaint Free World*

Meditation

Eknath Easwaran, *Conquest of Mind*

Dr Herbert Benson and William Proctor, *Relaxation Revolution*

Jon Kabat-Zinn, *Wherever You Go There You Are*

Matthieu Ricard, *Why Meditate?*

Metaphysical (aka the stuff that science is yet to figure out)

Gregg Braden, *The Divine Matrix*

Paramahansa Yogananda, *Autobiography of a Yogi* *

The Mind–Body Connection

Dr Bruce Lipton, *The Biology of Belief* *

Dr Darren Weissman, *The Power of Infinite Love and Gratitude*

Louise Hay, *You Can Heal Your Life*

Movie: *What the Bleep Do We Know?*

Motivation, Inspiration and Peak Performance

Anthony Robbins, *Awaken the Giant Within*

Brian Johnson, *A Philosopher's Notes on Optimal Living*

Carol Dweck, *Mindset* *

Darren Hardy, *The Compound Effect*

Don Miguel Ruiz, *The Four Agreements* *

Dr Heidi Halvorson, *Succeed*

Jack Canfield, *The Success Principles*

Michael Gelb, *How to Think Like Leonardo Da Vinci*

Robin Sharma, *The Monk who Sold his Ferrari*

Steven Pressfield, *The War of Art* *

Nutrition

Dr Colin T Campbell, *The China Study* *

Gene Stone, *Forks over Knives*

Dr Joel Fuhrman, MD, *Eat To Live* *

Mike Anderson, *The Rave Diet and Lifestyle*

Physical Activity

Christopher McDougall, *Born to Run*

John R Little and Doug McGuff, *Body by Science*

Rich Roll, *Finding Ultra* *

Psychology

Albert Ellis, *Overcoming Destructive Beliefs, Feelings and Behaviors*

Martin Seligman, *Learned Optimism*

Spirituality

Deepak Chopra, *The Seven Spiritual Laws of Success*

Eckhart Tolle, *A New Earth*

Hermann Hesse, *Siddhartha* *

Wayne Dwyer, *Wisdom of the Ages*

Wealth

Brendon Burchard, *The Millionaire Messenger*

M J DeMarco, *The Millionaire Fastlane* *

Napoleon Hill, *Think and Grow Rich*

Retreats

Hemingways Journeys

Owned by Adelle Hemingway, Hemingways Journeys works with a family-run professional trekking company in Nepal, which specializes in creating tailor-made and unique travel experiences, specific to your availability, ability and the style of journey you have in mind. Whether you are 8 or 80 years old, the expert guidance and personal support that Hemingways Journeys provides ensures that everyone has an amazing and memorable experience from the first step in Nepal to the very last. They also run yoga and trekking tours in Nepal and Bhutan, which bring like-minded people together for a transformative experience that is both energizing and cleansing for the body and mind.

My trek with Hemingways Journeys was one of my favorite adventures in 2011. It felt like a naturally occurring physical and mental detox, which had me re-energized and rejuvenated at the end. I enjoyed a highly beneficial experience with a group of friends and helpful guides and porters.

www.hemingwaysjourneys.com

Epic Private Journeys

This luxury adventure travel operator offers incomparable tailored journeys to Africa, Australia, Bhutan, India, Papua New Guinea, New Zealand, Peru, Chile and the US South-West. Owned by Brad Horn (an ex-Australian Army colleague), Epic is a very professional and fun business taking in some of the most amazing locations on the planet.

www.epicprivatejourneys.com

Embracing Life! Six & Eight Day Detox, Healing & Raw Food Retreats

Embracing Health offers transforming experiences where participants are empowered with the knowledge and inspiration to make changes in their lives that lead to better physical, emotional and spiritual health. Leisa Wheeler, naturopath and founder of Embracing Health, provides a specialized health program, delivering high-quality education combined with massage, yoga, gourmet raw vegan food, meditation and food preparation classes in beautiful settings across Australia and in Bali.

www.embracinghealth.com/retreat/

Acknowledgments

My biggest thanks go to my partner, Ferry Tan, who has been a big part of me being true to my teachings and has had to field more than her fair share of questions (and interruptions) as I think aloud, or ponder the deeper meaning of the material I read and research. She is also the creative force behind all of my work with her company, *Invisible Resources*, and her amazing talent. The book cover, I think, is absolutely amazing.

I am also grateful for finding an amazing editor and supporter in Desanka Vukelich from *For The Love Of Words*. I love the synchronicity at work with how we got connected and how your schedule just opened up for me at the right time. Meant to be.

None of this would have been possible without a certain guy and girl falling in love many, many moons ago. So to mum and dad; thank you so much for getting me through the first part of my life in one piece, with a great set of values and a healthy dose of curiosity to explore this wonderful journey called life. To my brother and sister - thanks a lot for a colorful, exciting and fun learning environment for my formative years. May the formative years never end. ;-)

A big thanks goes out to all my amazing friends, family, colleagues, ex-Defence buddies, Games crew, clients and associates that I have had the joy and good fortune to have in my life over the last 43 years. If I have offended any of you over the years, please take this as a formal apology and I will endeavor to improve along the way. Thanks for the help and support over the years in deepening my understanding about life and myself in general. I learn from each and every one of you.

And finally thank you to all of the amazing authors, researchers, teachers, thought-leaders and visionaries that have been a major part of my education over the years. The knowledge we now have access to from past and present teachers is unprecedented and thank you to them for having the courage and good grace to share what they learned. Thanks!

Copyright